Time & Money

By
Bill Linderman

Cover Illustration
by
Laura Zarrin

Inside Illustrations
by
Tim Foley

Publishers
Instructional Fair • TS Denison
Grand Rapids, Michigan 49544

About the Author

Bill Linderman has a master's degree in Elementary Education from Arizona State University. He has taught for 19 years, and has written nearly 40 books for Instructional Fair and TS Denison.

Credits

Author: Bill Linderman
Cover Illustration: Laura Zarrin
Inside Illustration: Tim Foley
Project Director/Editor: Kathryn Wheeler
Editors: Linda Triemstra, Meredith Van Zomeren
Page Design: Pat Geasler
Cover Designer: Matthew Van Zomeren

Standard Book Number: 1-56822-905-4
Time & Money—Grades 2–3

a Tribune Education Company
3195 Wilson Ave. NW
Grand Rapids, Michigan 49544

    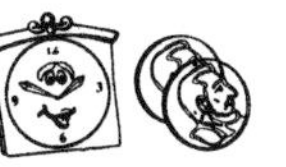  

Table of Contents

Time

Money

Name ______________________

Time to Talk Time!

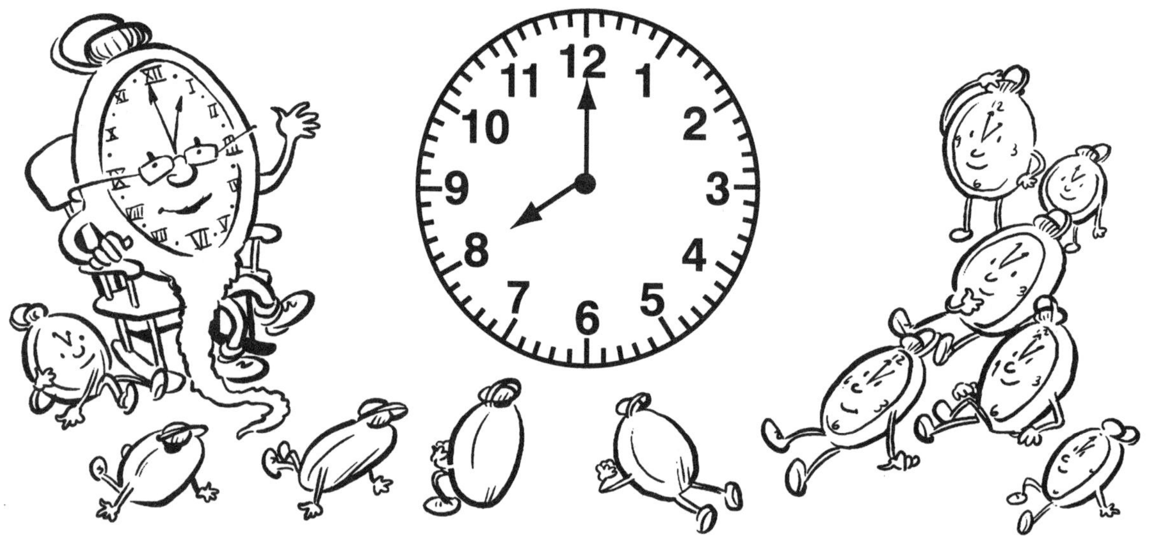

Circle the correct answer.

1. The little hand tells us what ______ it is. **minute hour**
2. The big hand tells us how many ______ have passed after the hour. **minutes hours**
3. There are ______ minutes in between each number on the face of the clock. **1 5 10**
4. If the minute hand is on the **1**, that means it is ______ minutes past the hour. **5 10 15**
5. If the minute hand is on the **3**, that means that it is ______ minutes past the hour. **10 15 30 45**
6. If the minute hand is on the **9**, that means that it is ______ minutes past the hour. **10 15 30 45**
7. If the minute hand is on the **6**, that means that it is ______ minutes past the hour. **10 15 30 45**

Name ______________________

Complete the statement below. Fill in each blank with the word that matches the hour on the clock below.

Learning to tell time is very important! So, ________ (9:00) out your ________ (6:00), ________ (11:00), ________ (4:00) timepiece, and learn to ________ (2:00) ________ (12:00)!

tin

tilted

tell

tiny

tinted

time

take

terrible

Name ____________________

Clockman

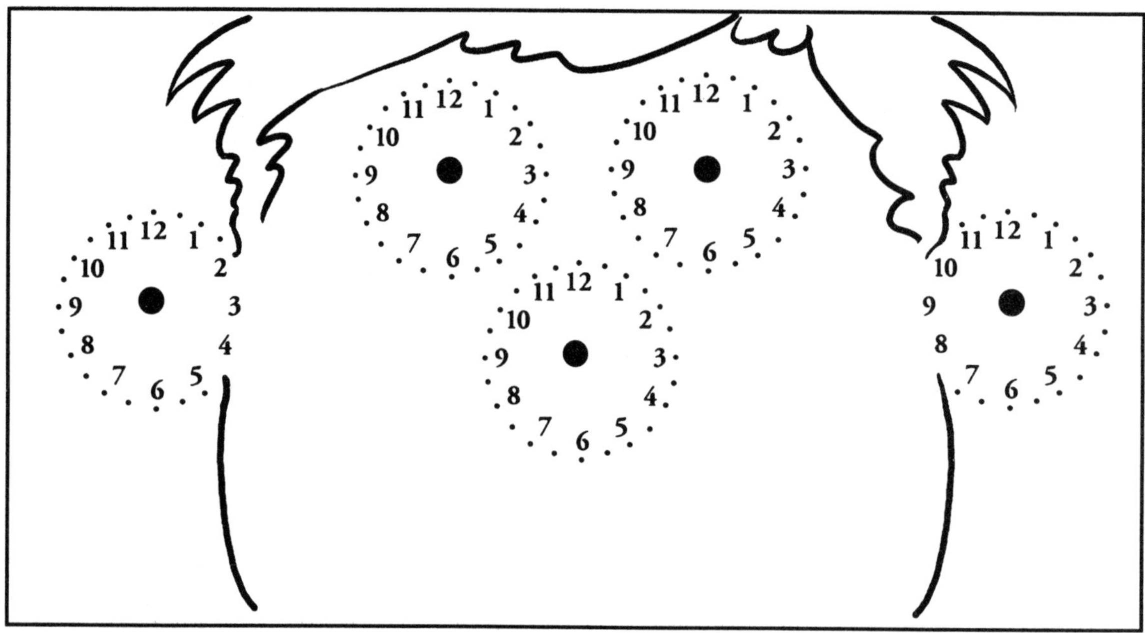

Clockman's right side

Clockman's left side

Follow the directions.

1. Trace the circles that will be Clockman's eyes.
2. Trace the circle that will be Clockman's nose.
3. Trace the circles that will be Clockman's ears.
4. Draw clock hands in Clockman's left eye that read 3 o'clock.
5. Draw clock hands in Clockman's right eye that read 9 o'clock.
6. Draw clock hands in Clockman's left ear that read 8 o'clock.
7. Draw clock hands in Clockman's right ear that read 4 o'clock.
8. Draw clock hands in Clockman's nose that read 6 o'clock.
9. Draw a big smile on Clockman's face!

Name ______________________

Clockman never forgets certain times because they are right there on his face. Look at his face on page 6 to write the correct times.

10. Clockman's school ends at the time shown in his left eye. ____ : ____

11. Clockman's school starts at the time shown in his left ear. ____ : ____

12. Clockman's dinner time is on his nose! ____ : ____

13. Clockman's piano lesson starts at the time shown in his right ear.
    ____ : ____

14. If Clockman's piano lesson lasts one hour, what time does it end?
    ____ : ____

15. Clockman does his time homework for an hour after dinner. If his dinner ends at 7 o'clock, what time does Clockman finish his homework?
    ____ : ____

16. If Clockman goes to bed an hour after his homework is done, what is his bedtime?____ : ____

Name ______________________

Halfway Around the Clock

The big hand is on the six when the time is half past the hour. If the little hand points near the 9, and the big hand points to the 6, what time is it?

_____ : _____

Write these times.

_____ : _____

_____ : _____

_____ : _____

When the minute hand is halfway around the clock, that's a half-hour. A half-hour is 30 minutes long. That's why we write 5:30 for half past 5.

Write the times.

1. A half-hour past 12 o'clock is _____ : _____ .
2. A half-hour past 8 o'clock is _____ : _____ .
3. 6:30 is a half-hour after _____ : _____ .
4. 2:30 is a half-hour past _____ : _____ .
5. 5:30 is a half-hour past _____ : _____ .
6. 10:30 is a half-hour past _____ : _____ .
7. 2:00 is a half-hour before _____ : _____ .
8. 8:00 is a half-hour before _____ : _____ .

Name ______________________

The Hidden Half-Hour Puzzle

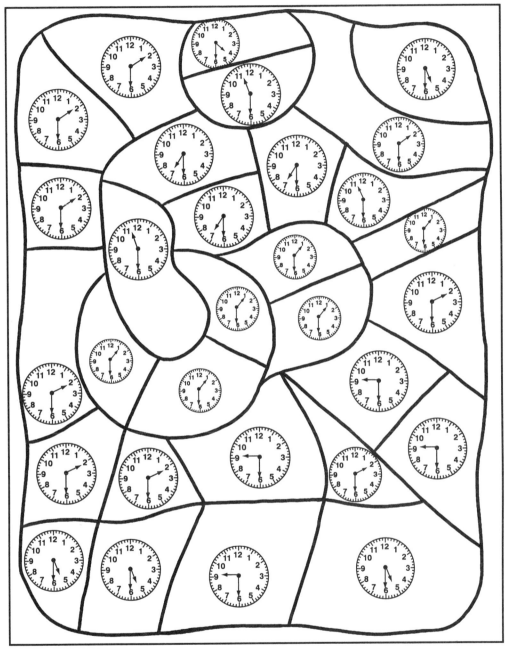

Color this puzzle using this key:

If the clock says . . .

7:30, color the shape red.

2:30, color the shape purple.

5:30, color the shape yellow.

4:30, color the shape green.

9:30, color the shape blue

11:30, color the shape orange

1:30, color the shape brown

Name ______________________________

Quarters of an Hour

One-fourth of an hour is 15 minutes. Each time the minute hand moves 15 minutes, we call that a "quarter-hour."

Count by 5s to find each quarter-hour time.

The last quarter-hour is the new hour!

This is a quarter past the hour, or 12:15.

5
10
15
20
25
30

This is half past the hour, or 12:30.

This is three-quarters past the hour, or 12:45.

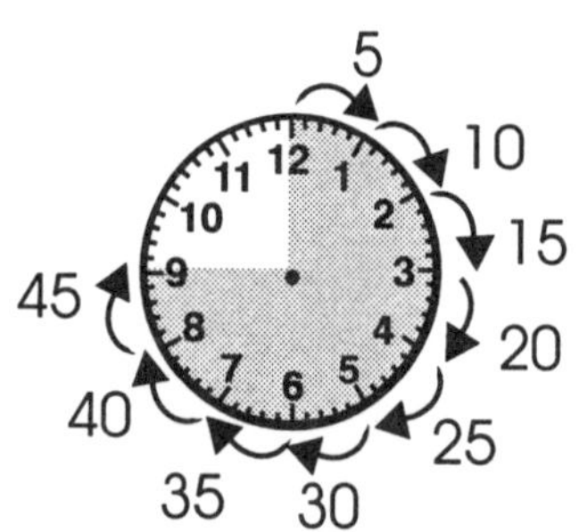

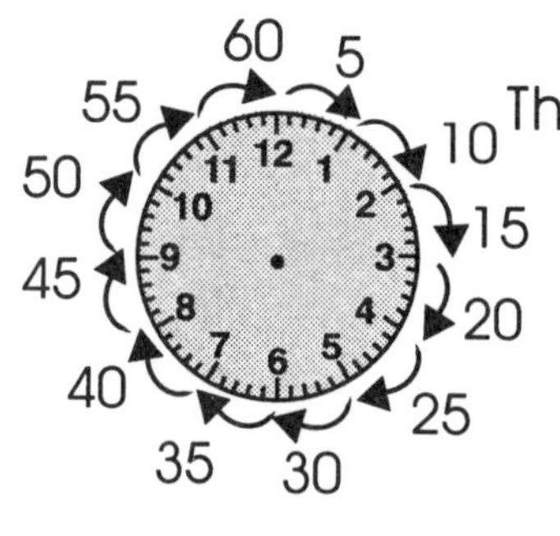

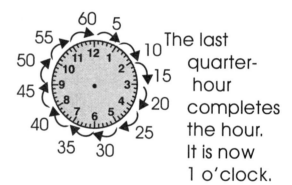

The last quarter-hour completes the hour. It is now 1 o'clock.

Place the minute hand on each clock to show the quarter-hours.

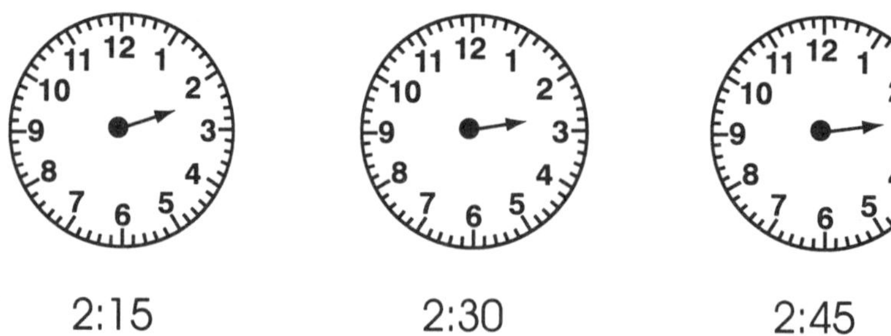

2:15 2:30 2:45

The final quarter hour would be: **2:50 3:00 3:05**

Name ______________________

Stops and Starts

1. Billy had a great time doing chalk drawings in the driveway at 2:15. It rained 15 minutes later! What time did the chalk drawings vanish?

   ____

2. Carrie loves to rollerblade. She went outside with her friends at 3:00. At 3:30 they came back inside. For how many minutes did they skate?

   ____

3. Mark and his mother went outside to look at the stars through their telescope. It started getting dark at 7:00. By 8:00 they went inside. How long were they looking at stars? ____________________

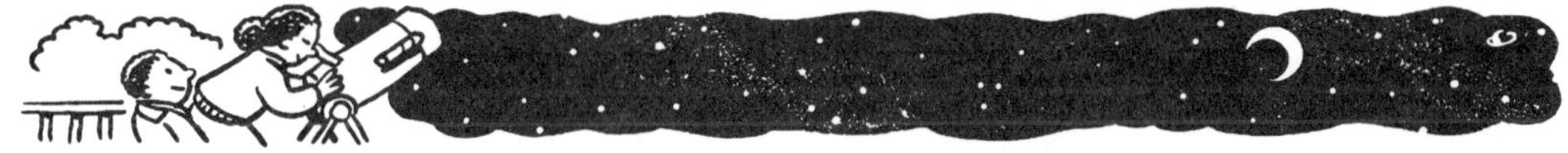

4. Tasha's new kitten loves to play with a ball of yarn. But by 4:30 she was fast asleep in Tasha's lap. The kitten played with the yarn for a quarter-hour. What time did she start? __________

5. Eva and her father worked on a model rocket together. The fins were hard to attach. By 11:30, they had worked on the fins for a half-hour. What time did they begin? __________

Name ______________________

Quarter-Hours in Flight

Each quarter-hour takes up one-quarter of a clock's face.

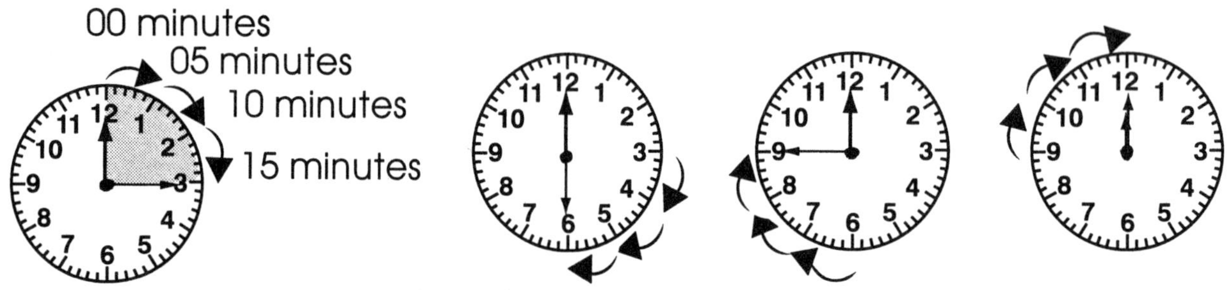

A quarter-hour is 15 minutes. There are 5 minutes between each number on the face of the clock. So when the big hand moves from 12 to 3, it has moved a quarter-hour, which is 15 minutes!

Draw the minute hand on each clock to show a quarter past the hour. Write the time in the blank below.

Write the times:

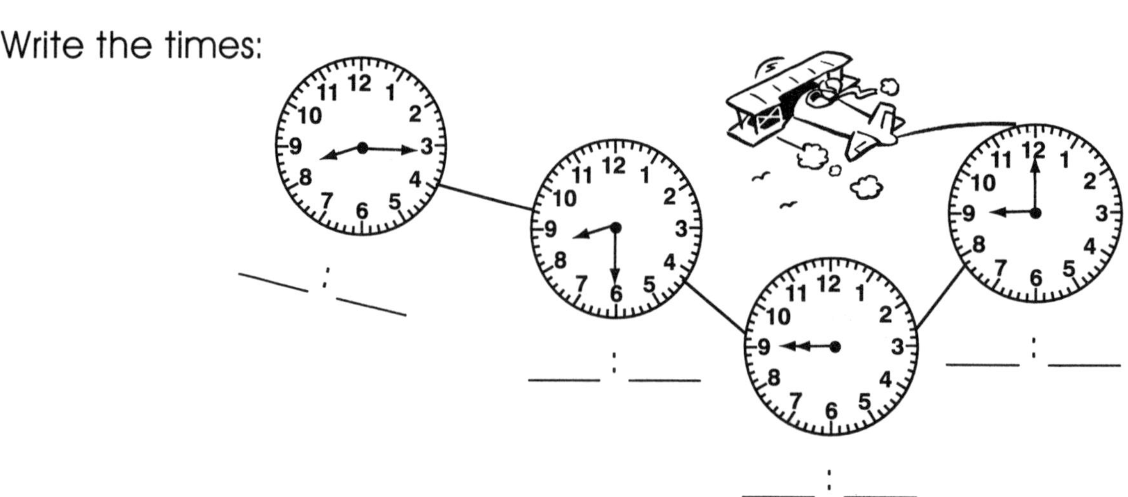

Name ______________________

Time is really "flying by" here! Identify each quarter-hour as it flies by. Write the correct time in each blank.

_____ : _____

_____ : _____

_____ : _____

_____ : _____

_____ : _____

_____ : _____

_____ : _____

_____ : _____

Quarter-hour time!

Name ______________________

Quarter-Hour Clues

Sherlock Squirrel needs to find the trail of the Quarter-Hour Bandit! Help him write each time. Then figure out the time for one quarter-hour later.

Time: ___ : ___   ___ : ___   ___ : ___

15 minutes later:

___ : ___   ___ : ___   ___ : ___

Time: ___ : ___   ___ : ___   ___ : ___

15 minutes later:

___ : ___   ___ : ___   ___ : ___

Name ______________________

Help Sherlock Squirrel through this quarter-hour course to find the bandit hideout! Look at the time on each clock. Write the time for a quarter-hour **later** in each box.

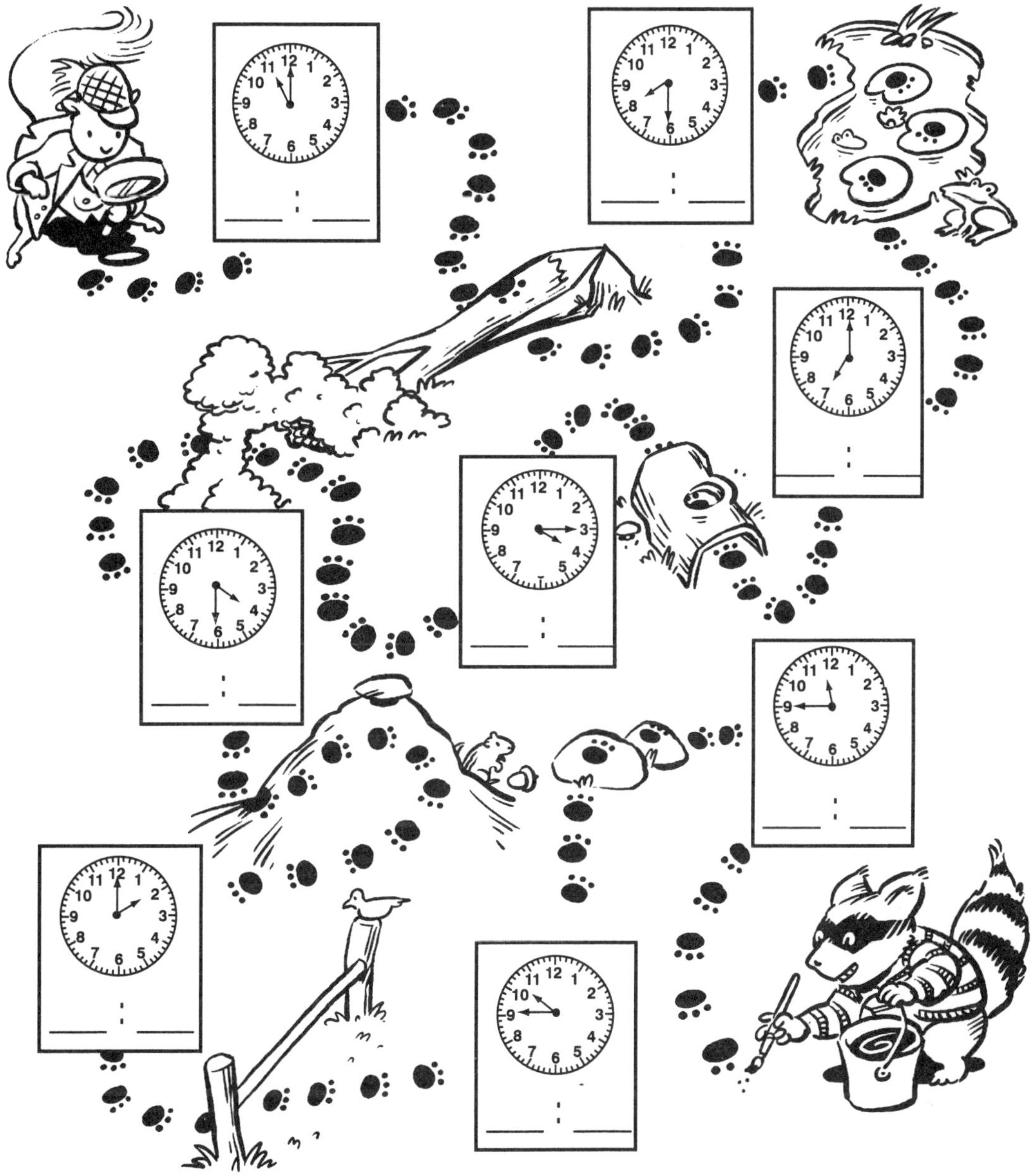

____ : ____

____ : ____

____ : ____

____ : ____

____ : ____

____ : ____

____ : ____

____ : ____

Name ______________________

Quarter-Hour Art Class

Read the story problems. Then write the correct times in the blanks.

1. In art class, Mark started drawing a ranch at 1:00. It took him a quarter-hour to draw a horse. What time did he finish his horse? _____ : _____
2. The teacher told Chung to wait a quarter-hour to let the glue dry on her collage. She started working again at 1:30. What time did she stop to let the glue dry? _____ : _____

3. David spilled some paint, and it took him a quarter-hour to clean it up. He started cleaning at 1:30. What time did he finish? _____ : _____
4. Martha was asked to help pick up art supplies. She got everything put away by 2:00. It took her a quarter-hour. What time did she start? _____ : _____

Name ______________________

Now it's time for your art class! Color the shapes with each time. Use the key to pick each color.

Key

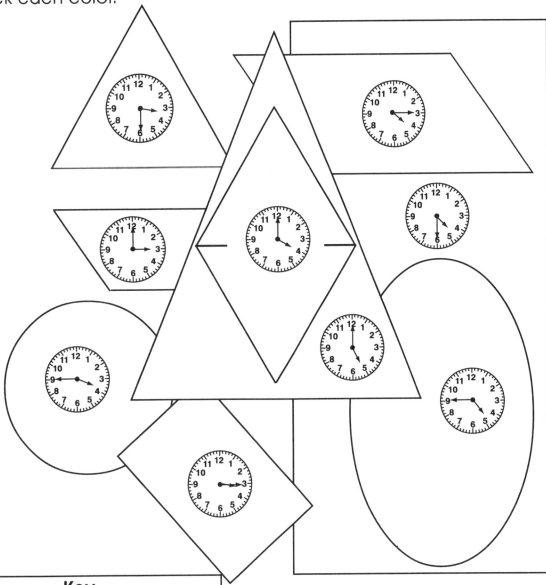

3:00 = red	3:15 = green
3:30 = purple	3:45 = blue
4:00 = yellow	4:15 = orange
4:30 = pink	4:45 = brown
5:00 = black	

Name ______________________

Bubble Fun!

The bubble fun starts at 12:00. Jump from bubble to bubble, and fill in each quarter-hour as you go!

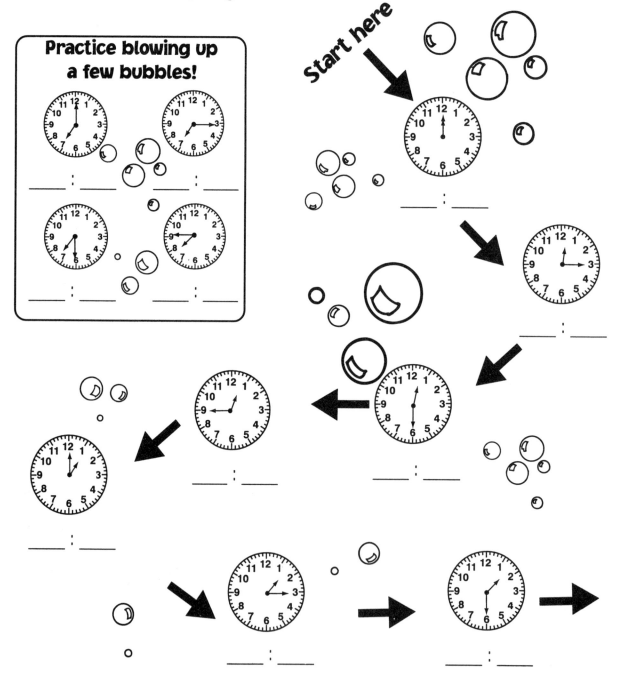

Practice blowing up a few bubbles!

____ : ____ ____ : ____

____ : ____ ____ : ____

Start here

____ : ____

____ : ____

____ : ____

____ : ____

____ : ____

____ : ____

____ : ____

Name ____________________

Fill in each quarter-hour as you jump from bubble to bubble.

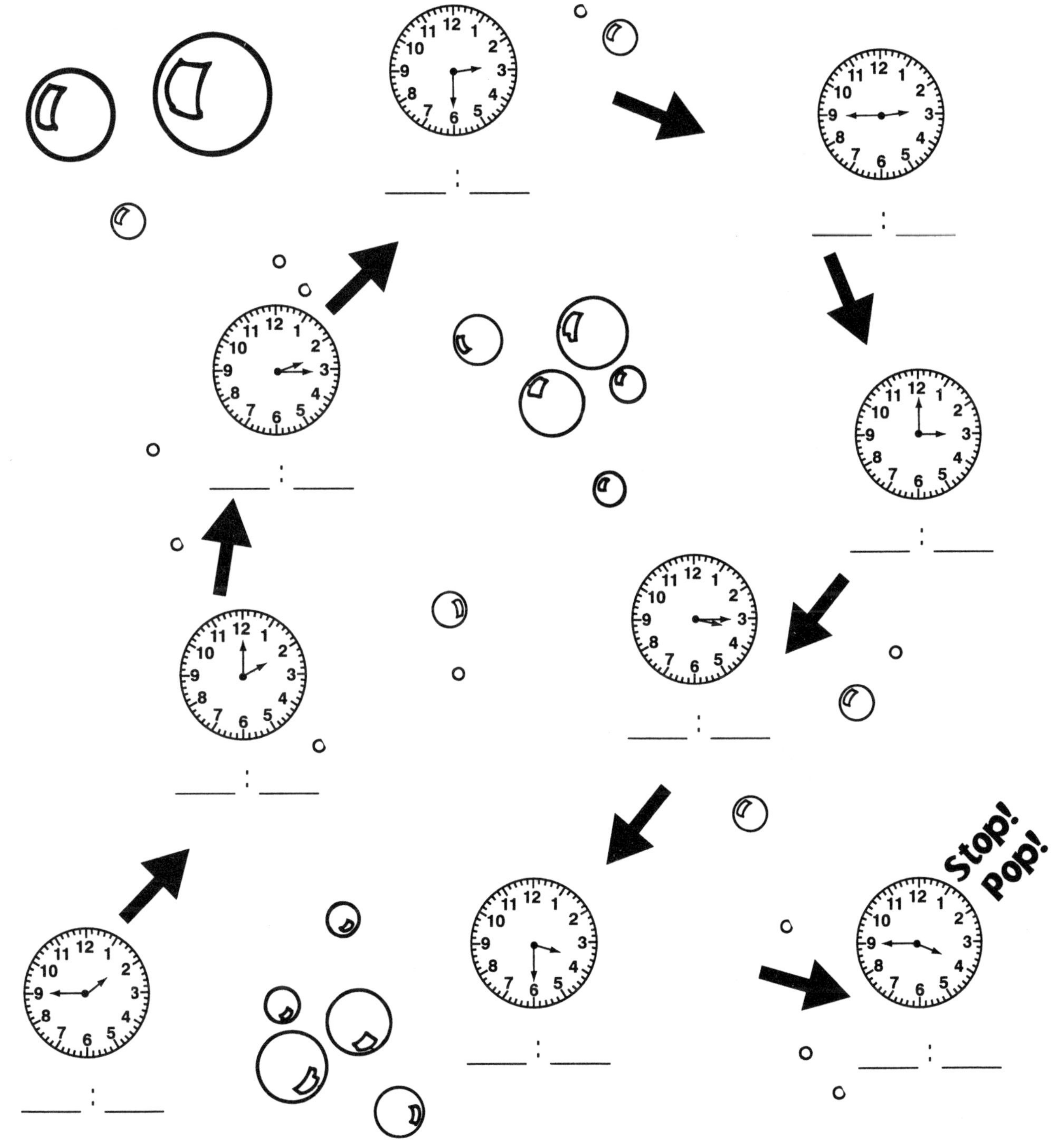

___ : ___

___ : ___

___ : ___

___ : ___

___ : ___

___ : ___

___ : ___

___ : ___

Stop! Pop!

Name ____________________

Five Is the Key

It takes five minutes for the minute hand to move from one number to another. Start at the 12 and count by 5s.

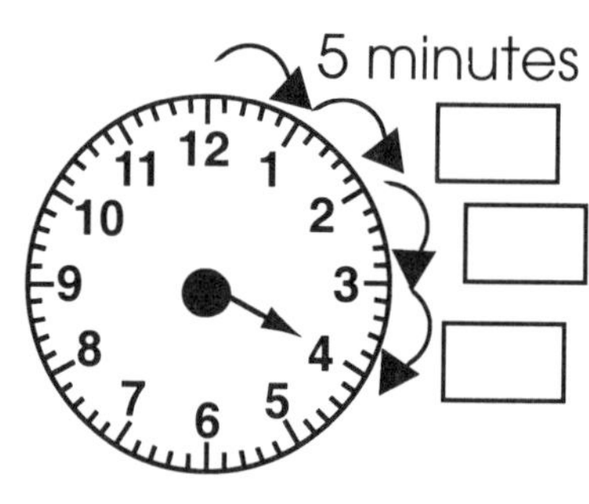

You can read minutes easily by counting by 5s. For example, when the minute hand is on the 4, it's 20 minutes past the hour.

Count by 5s. Write the minutes under each clock.

3 : ____

10 : ____

12 : ____

8 : ____

12 : ____

9 : ____

Name ____________________

Adding Up the Minutes

Help Chung keep track of time. Write the correct time beneath each clock.

1. Chung leaves her house at 9:00. It takes her 10 minutes to walk to Maria's house. What time does she arrive?

_____ : _____

2. Maria shows Chung the new kittens. They play with the kittens for 25 minutes. What time do they stop?

_____ : _____

3. Then Maria and Chung go outside to play in Maria's swimming pool. They swim for 45 minutes. What time do they get out of the pool?

_____ : _____

4. Chung and Maria walk to their school to play on the playground. They leave at 10:45. It takes them 5 minutes to walk to the school. What time do they arrive?

_____ : _____

Name ____________________

Time Travel

Every day, we travel through time! Follow Alesha through her day. Write each time.

Alesha gets on her bike at ___ : ___ .

Five minutes later, she is at her grandfather's house. ___ : ___

Today is a special day. It's Grandpa's birthday! He opens his card at ___ : ___.

Grandpa takes Alesha out to breakfast at ___ : ___.

Since it's his birthday, Grandpa orders pan<u>cakes</u>!

Name ______________________

Time Travel Too

Write the times as David writes his story!

David sits down to write a new story at
____ : ____.

He is writing a story about puppies. David writes for 15 minutes. ____ : ____

David feels a tug on his jeans. He
pretends not to notice for 5 minutes, until ____ : ____.

It's his new puppy, Chiggles! David
decides to play with her for a half-hour,
until ____ : ____.

Name ____________________

Time for School

Help Eva plan her school day.

Eva walks to school. School begins at ____ : ____ .

Draw a line to the correct time for each class.

Reading starts one hour after school begins.

Lunch is two hours after the start of reading.

Math begins one hour after the beginning of lunch.

Social studies begins three hours after the start of lunch.

Name ____________________

Fun Day

Each person here spent one hour at a Fun Day activity. They started at different times. Write the times when they were done in the spaces.

Sam went on the bumper car ride from 1:00 to ____ : ____ .

Pedro started playing hockey at 1:30. He was done at ____ : ____ .

Eva rode a unicycle! She rode from 3:00 to ____ : ____ .

Chung made chalk drawings from 2:30 to ___ : ___.

David played marbles from 2:15 to ____ : ____.

Name ______________________________

School Picnic Time

Join the school picnic! You can be the timekeeper.

Calculate how much time each activity took. Write your answers in the blanks.

1. David and Anna May played volleyball from 1:20 till 1:40. They played ______ minutes.

2. Alesha rode a pony for 25 minutes. She began at 1:00. She finished at ____ : ____ .

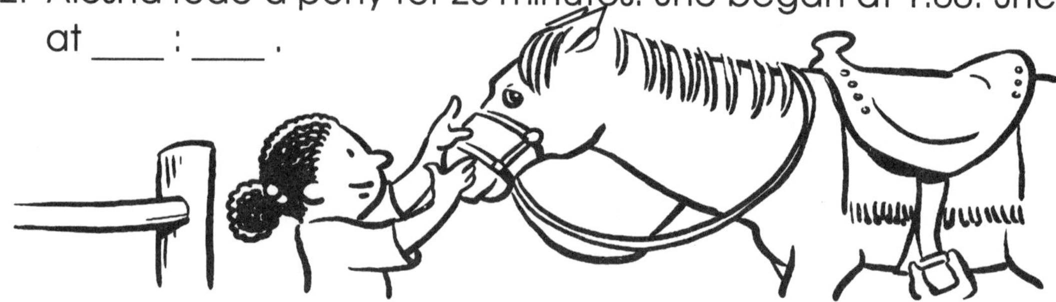

3. Alesha had so much fun that she stayed for another 15 minutes! She finished her second pony ride at ____ : ____ .

Name ______________________________

4. Mark worked at the snack bar. The first clock shows the time he started working. He worked 1 hour and 30 minutes. Show the time he finished on the second clock.

5. Chung won the juggling contest! She kept the balls in the air for 5 minutes! She began juggling at 1:30 . She finished at ____ : _____ . Circle the clock which shows the correct time that Chung finished juggling.

Write the times shown on each clock.

_____ : _____	_____ : _____	_____ : _____	_____ : _____
Eva wins a track prize.	The baseball game ends.	The bus heads back to school.	Everyone goes home.

Name ______________________

Break the Codes!

Can you read these secret messages? You can if you can read the time!

Write the correct time under each clock. Then match the letter of that clock to a space below. When all the blanks are filled in, read the message!

Question:
Who will tell if you are late?

L = ___:___

E = ___:___

T = ___:___

! = ___:___

M = ___:___

W = ___:___

I = ___:___

___ ___ ___ ___
6:05 8:40 3:25 7:25

___ ___ ___ ___
4:10 8:40 8:15 8:15

___ ___ ___ ___ ___
6:05 7:25 8:15 8:15 11:55

Name ____________________

Write the correct time under each clock. Then match the letter of each clock to a space below.

Question:

How do we know that time is as light as air?

E = ___:___

L = ___:___

T = ___:___

M = ___:___

I = ___:___

F = ___:___

E = ___:___

S = ___:___

I = ___:___

Because

___	___	___	___
6:40	12:00	3:45	4:55

___	___	___	___	___.
10:30	7:55	7:25	1:00	9:15

Name ____________________

Time Never Stops

Let's say that it is 1:00. Thirty minutes from now it will be 1:30. Thirty minutes from 1:30, it will be 2:00. Time keeps moving. Write the time shown on the clock face. Then write the time a half-hour earlier or later, as shown.

____ : ____ + 30 minutes

= ____ : ____

____ : ____ + 30 minutes

= ____ : ____

____ : ____ - 30 minutes

= ____ : ____

____ : ____ + 30 minutes

= ____ : ____

____ : ____ + 30 minutes

= ____ : ____

____ : ____ - 30 minutes

= ____ : ____

How many minutes are there in each half-hour?

15 30 60

Name ______________________

Game Time

This is "Tick, Tack, Clock"! To win this game, find three clocks that are showing quarter-hours! Write each time. Find the three quarter-hour clocks and draw a line right through them!

____ : ____	____ : ____	____ : ____
____ : ____	____ : ____	____ : ____
____ : ____	____ : ____	____ : ____

Name ____________________

Welcome to Class!

Here are all the things that happened in a classroom today. Keep track of time as it passes by writing down the correct time after each event.

1. Class started when Mrs. Andrews introduced the new class pet! **8:00** The students spent 10 minutes meeting Jerry the Gerbil. What time were they done? _____ : _____

2. Martha shared a book with the class about colorful animals that live around the world. **9:00**

   It took Martha 20 minutes to show her book to everyone. When did they finish? _____ : _____

3. Monica shared birthday treats with her class. Everyone loved them! **10:15**

   The class finished the treats in 10 minutes. What time were they done? _____ : _____

4. Eva gave her report on frogs during science. **11:00**

   Eva took 15 minutes to give her report. When did she finish? _____ : _____

Name ______________________

5. David worked on a fort outside during recess. **1:30**

   Recess was 20 minutes. What time did David stop?

   _____ : _____

6. Pedro painted a picture of his house during art class. He used colored sand to cover the outside. **2:00**

   Pedro worked on his picture for 40 minutes. What time was he done?

   _____ : _____

7. Chung made a reed flute during art class. She wrapped it in paper to take it home. **2:55**

   Chung was ready to catch the bus in 5 minutes. What time did she finish wrapping her flute? _____ : _____

8. If Chung's bus ride home took 15 minutes, what time did she get home?

   _____ : _____

Name ____________________

Chart It!

On the planet Zotz, Mrs. Bleepz has made a chart to help her remember her children's schedules. Read the chart. Then answer the questions on page 35.

	Blurp	**Zeezo**	**Bleeza**
Ride transport to school	7:30	8:00	8:15
Home from school	3:15	4:00	3:45
Zeek-X practice	4:30	—	4:45
Flugle lesson	—	4:30	5:30
Starts homework	5:30	7:30	7:00

Name ____________________

Write the time.

1. When does Blurp ride the transport? _____ : _____

2. When does Bleeza get home from school? _____ : _____

3. What time does Zeezo go to his flugle lesson? _____ : _____

4. If Bleeza has an hour of homework, what time will she be done? _____ : _____

5. What time does Zeezo start his homework?_____ : _____

Circle the right answer.

6. Who goes to a flugle lesson first?

   Blurp Zeezo Bleeza

7. Who gets home first?

   Blurp Zeezo Bleeza

8. Who plays Zeek-X at 4:30?

   Blurp Zeezo Bleeza

9. Who rides the transport first?

   Blurp Zeezo Bleeza

10. Who rides the transport last?

   Blurp Zeezo Bleeza

Do you see why Mrs. Bleepz needs a chart?

Name ______________________

Just a Minute!

How long is a minute? It zooms by! Circle each activity that only takes one minute.

Name ____________________

A Minute at a Time

If the minute hand points to the first mark right after the **12**, that means it is 1 minute past the hour.

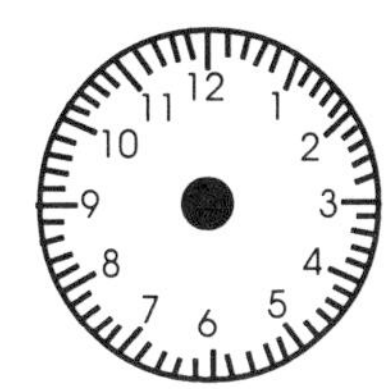

If the minute hand points to the mark right after the **1**, that means it is 5 minutes + 1 minute past the hour, or ______ minutes.

If the minute hand points to the mark right after the **2**, that means it is ______ minutes past the hour.

Try these:

_____ minutes after the hour .

_____ minutes after the hour .

_____ minutes after the hour.

Name ________________________

Digital Minutes!

It is easier to tell time to the minute on a digital clock face. If the digital clock read 12:06, that means it is 6 minutes past 12. A digital clock counts minutes for you.

Draw a line from each clock on the left to a clock on the right that is one minute later.

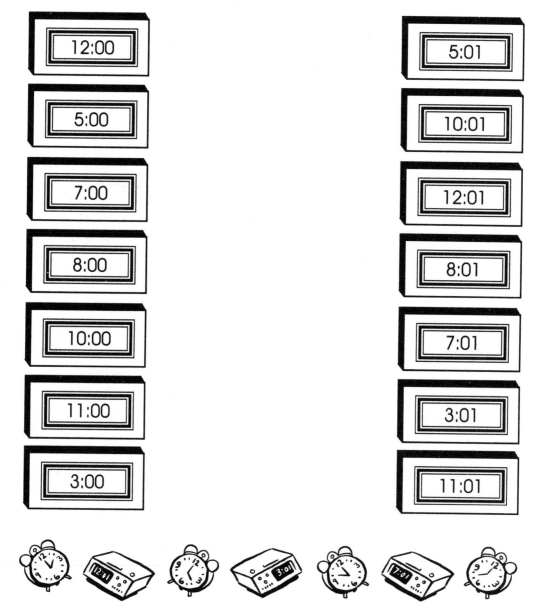

12:00	5:01
5:00	10:01
7:00	12:01
8:00	8:01
10:00	7:01
11:00	3:01
3:00	11:01

Name ______________________

One Minute Later

Write the correct times.

1. It takes Mark one minute to run from the basement to the attic. If he starts at 1:06, what time will he get to the attic?

   _____ : _____

2. At 6:02, Maria's mother calls out, "The pizza is here!" Her brothers are there a minute later, at _____ : _____ .

3. David's father backs the car out. It takes him a minute to stop the car and close the garage door. If he starts at 4:29, when are they on their way? _____ : _____

4. Chung can draw a picture of a rabbit in one minute. She starts at 10:09. What time is she done?

   _____ : _____

5. The bus picks up Eva at 7:47. If she is a minute early, what time does she get to her bus stop?

   _____ : _____

Name ____________________

Early, Late, or On Time?

Imagine you are going to a birthday party. It starts at 2:00.

If you arrive at the party at 2:00, we say you are "on time."

If you arrive **before** 2:00, you are **early**.

If you arrive after 2:00, you are **late**.

Circle the correct time.

Kim eats dinner at 5:30. Circle the clock that shows a time when dinner at her house was **early**.

Circle the correct answer: If Kim's dinner is served on time, and she got home from Girl Scouts at 5:40, would she be

early **late** **on time**

Name ____________________

Are They On Time?

Circle the correct times.

1. Chung goes to her piano lesson at 4:00. Circle the clock that shows she was **on time**.

2. David's school starts at 8:00. Circle the clock that shows he was **late**.

3. Maria feeds her kitten at 7:00. Circle the clock that shows she was **early**.

4. Earl had to go to the dentist at 3:15. Circle the clock that shows he was **on time**.

Name ______________________

7 Days = 1 Week

Let's see how much you know about the days of the week!

Sunday	Monday	Tuesday	Wednesday	Thursday	Friday	Saturday
1	2	3	4	5	6	7

1. Circle the first day of the week:

   Sunday   Monday   Thursday   Wednesday

2. Circle the last day of the week:

   Friday   Saturday

3. Which day has the most letters in its name?

   ____

4. The hour hand goes all the way around the clock twice during one day. How many hours are there in one day? ________

5. Which two days make up the weekend?

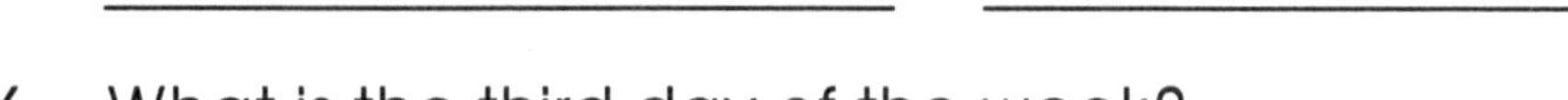

6. What is the third day of the week?

   ____

7. Write the name of your favorite day of the week:

   ____

Name ______________________

All in One Week

Fill in each blank below. Use the clue to find each day of the week.

1. Earl plays soccer on ______________________.
   (sixth day)

2. Monica has dance class every ______________________.
   (third day)

3. Pedro rides his bike to the park on ______________________.
   (seventh day)

4. Maria has swimming lessons on ______________________.
   (fifth day)

5. Tammy never misses choir practice on ______________________.
   (fourth day)

6. Jacob's first day of school was ______________________.
   (second day)

Name ____________________

Name That Day!

Many of the names we give to the days of the week come from old myths, stories, and the stars! Let's see if you can guess these names. Circle each correct answer.

1. One day of the week is named for Thor, who made thunder with his giant hammer. Is it:

   Monday   Thursday   Tuesday

2. The Romans named one day after Saturn. Is it:

   Sunday   Wednesday   Saturday

3. Odin ruled Valhalla in Norse stories. Is his day:

   Monday   Wednesday   Tuesday

   Hint: His name was also spelled "Wodin."

4. In French, most of the days of the week end with "di." Find the French word for "Thursday":

   sàbado   jeudi   Woensdag

5. In Spanish, "moon" is "luna." Which day is named after the moon?

   domingo   martes   lunes

6. In English, Sunday is named for the sun, and another day is named for the moon. Is it:

   Monday   Wednesday   Tuesday

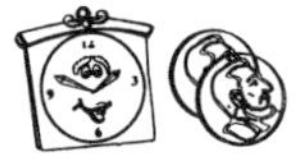      

Name ______________________________

Isabel's First Week

Write the correct days of the week in each blank to complete the story. Use the clues to help you.

The new baby was born on (third day) _______________ . The next day, (fourth day) __________________ , we decided to name her Isabel.

Mom and Isabel came home from the hospital on (fifth day) _________________________ . Two days later, (seventh day), _________________________ everybody came over to meet her!

Aunt Silvia and Uncle Frank had flown from Portland the day before, on (sixth day) _________________ . Grandma and Grandpa came over. So did Uncle Joe, and my cousins Rose and Robert.

I guess Isabel got tired out from all the people. On the day after the party, (first day) ____________________, she cried almost all morning!

She was better a day later, on (second day) ____________________ . That's when I brought Chung over to see my new sister. We made silly faces. Isabel smiled!

Name ____________________

Time for a Trip!

Eva's family is going on a vacation. Help them plan. Write the name of the day to show when they will reach each stop.

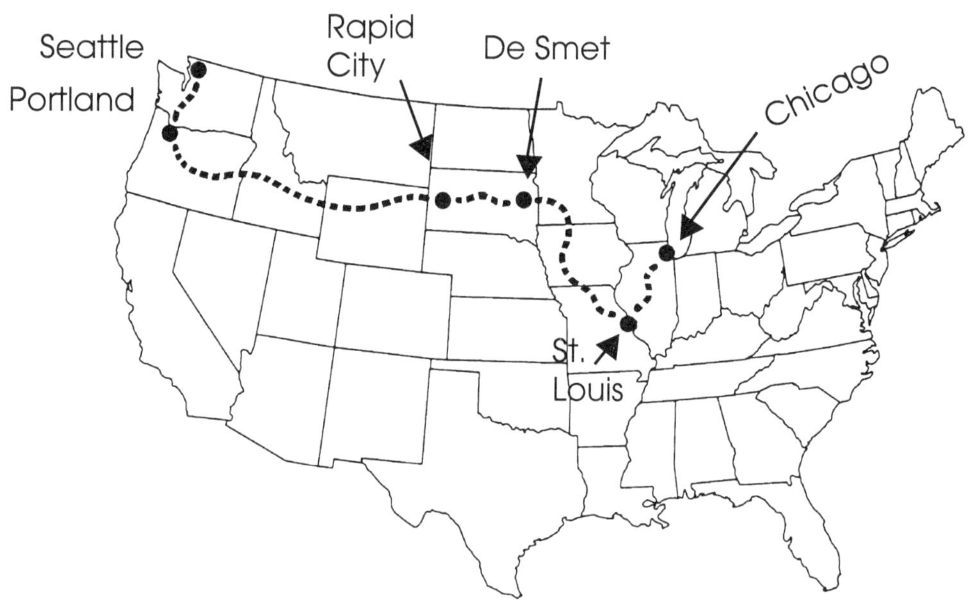

1. They leave from Seattle on

____________________.
(second day)

2. They visit Aunt May in Portland on

____________________.
(third day)

Name ______________________

Sunday	Monday	Tuesday	Wednesday	Thursday	Friday	Saturday
1	2	3	4	5	6	7

3. They go to Mount Rushmore near Rapid City on ______________________. (fifth day)

4. They see Laura Ingalls Wilder's home in De Smet on ______________________. (sixth day)

5. They take a riverboat tour in St. Louis on ______________________. (seventh day)

6. They go to a baseball game in Chicago on ______________________. (first day)

Eva thinks it's the best vacation her family has ever had!

Name ______________________________

All Year Long

January	February	March	April
BE MINE 1	2	3	4
May	**June**	**July**	**August**
5	6	7	8
September	**October**	**November**	**December**
9	10	11	12

Circle the correct answer.

1. January is the _______ month of the year.

   ninth   twelfth   first   second

2. December comes after _______________ .

   October   February   November   May

3. The month before September is ________________ .

   January   August   November   June

4. There are ________ months in every year.

   four   twelve   sixteen   eleven

5. July is a ____ month in the Northern Hemisphere.

   spring   summer   fall   winter

6. The third month of the year is

   February   March   May   March

Name ______________________

March

Sunday	Monday	Tuesday	Wednesday	Thursday	Friday	Saturday
	1	2	3	4	5	6
7	8	9	10	11	12	13
14	15	16	17	18	19	20
21	22	23	24	25	26	27
28	29	30	31			

Use the calendar page to answer the questions. Circle the correct answers.

1. The fourth day of March falls on what day of the week?

   Friday　　Monday　　Thursday　　Tuesday

2. What day does the tenth of March fall on?

   Monday　　Tuesday　　Wednesday　　Thursday

3. The first Saturday in March is March _____ .

   13　　27　　6　　20

4. The eleventh of March is the _____ Thursday in March.

   first　　second　　third　　fourth

5. The fourth Monday in March is March ______ .

   1　　8　　15　　22

6. How many Mondays are there in March?

   2　　5　　4　　6

Name ______________________

A Year of Months

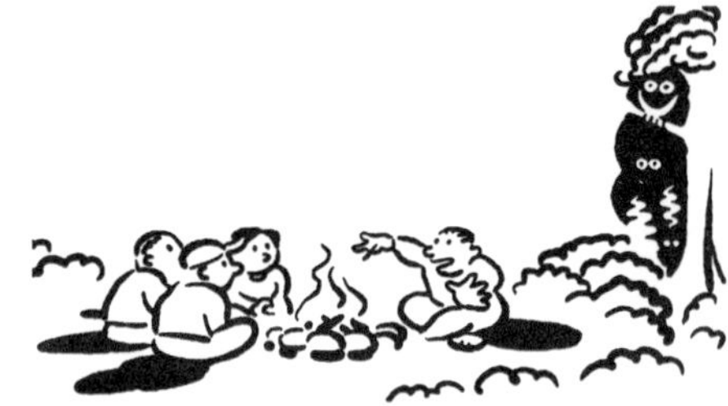

January **February** **March** **April** **May** **June**

July **August** **September** **October** **November** **December**

Write the month that comes before and after each month on the list.

1. ________________ September ________________
2. ________________ June ________________
3. ________________ December ________________
4. ________________ March ________________
5. ________________ August ________________
6. ________________ October ________________
7. ________________ February ________________
8. ________________ November ________________
9. What is the month before January? ______________

Name ______________________________

Every Month Is Magic

Complete each month sequence below.

1. January, February, March, ___________________ , May
2. May, _______________ ,July, _______________ ,September
3. February, March, ______________________ , May, June,

   _____________________ , _____________________

4. August, _____________________ , October, November,

   ______________________ , ___________________

Use the clues to complete each month.

1. School can start in this month.

   S ___ ___ t ___ ___ b ___ r

2. Parades and fireworks often start this month.

   ___ u ___ y

3. This month has 29 days in Leap Year.

   ___ e ___ r ___ ___ r y

4. Trees can lose their leaves during these fall months.

   O ___ ___ o ___ ___ r and ___ ov ___ ___ b ___ ___

Name ____________________

Let's Plan a Month

January						
Sunday	**Monday**	**Tuesday**	**Wednesday**	**Thursday**	**Friday**	**Saturday**
					1	**2** Concert
3 Family party for Chung	**4**	**5** Chung's birthday	**6**	**7**	**8**	**9** Maria's sledding party
10	**11** Teacher conference	**12**	**13**	**14**	**15**	**16**
17 Go to Grandma's for dinner	**18**	**19**	**20** Science Fair	**21**	**22**	**23**
24 / **31**	**25**	**26** Field trip	**27**	**28** Winter break	**29** Winter break	**30**

Here is Mrs. Lee's calendar for January. Use it to answer the questions. Circle the correct answers.

1. What day of the week is Chung's birthday?

   Sunday   Tuesday   Wednesday   Saturday

2. What is the date of the concert?

   January 2   January 4   January 5   January 6

3. What day of the week is Maria's sledding party?

   Friday   Saturday   Sunday   Monday

4. What is the date of Chung's field trip?

   January 21   January 26   January 30   January 25

5. What is the day of Chung's field trip?

   Monday   Tuesday   Wednesday   Thursday

Name ______________________

Write the answers to the questions. Use the calendar on page 52.

6. Write the date of the Science Fair. ______________________

7. What day of the week does Mrs. Lee have a teacher conference?
____

8. What day of the week is the Lee family going to Grandma's for dinner? ______________________

9. What is the date of Chung's birthday? ______________________

10. What day of the week is Chung's family giving her a party?
____

11. What are the two days of the week when Chung has winter break?
______________ and ______________

12. What is the date of Chung's last day of school before winter break?
____

13. On what day of the week does February start? ______________

Name ___________________________

It's Your Money!

Circle the correct answers.

1. Here's a penny.  It is worth _______ cent.

   1 **5** **10** **25** **50**

2. Remember the nickel?  It's worth ______ cents.

   1 **5** **10** **25** **50**

3. The smallest coin is the dime. 

   It is worth ______ cents.

   1 **5** **10** **25** **50**

4. The quarter is ¼ of a dollar, or ______ cents.

    **1** **5** **10** **25** **50**

5. The rare half-dollar  is worth ______ cents.

   1 **5** **10** **25** **50**

6. The dollar is paper.

   It is worth ________ cents.

   50 **100** **500** **1,000**

Name ______________________

Let's Trade

Did you know that you can trade one combination of money for another? Circle the correct amounts below.

1.  =      

2.  =   

3.  =    

4.  =       

5.  =    

6.  =   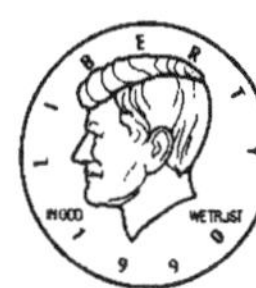 

Name ______________________

Let's Go to the Holiday Sale!

It's time for the holiday gift market at school! Count each student's money. Then use subtraction to see if he or she has enough money for each gift.

1. Kenny wants the telescope. He has:

_________ ¢

$-$ 95¢

Can he buy it?

Yes **No**

2. Trisha wants the puppet. She has:

_________ ¢

$-$ 85¢

Can she buy it?

Yes **No**

3. Monica wants the plant holder. She has:

_________ ¢

$-$ 45¢

Can she buy it?

Yes **No**

Name ____________________

4. Carrie wants the purse. She has:

_________ ¢

$-\ 50¢$

Can she buy it?

Yes **No**

5. Earl wants the puzzle. He has:

_________ ¢

$-\ 25¢$

Can he buy it?

Yes **No**

6. Janet wants the rabbit. She has:

_________ ¢

$-\ 75¢$

Can she buy it?

Yes **No**

7. Samuel has 45¢. Pick the **two** gifts he could buy if he spends all his money.

telescope 95¢	puppet 85¢	puzzle 25¢
bracelet 10¢	airplane 35¢	purse 50¢
yo-yo 40¢	plant holder 45¢	

Name ______________________________

A Coin Bigger Than a Quarter!

This is the half-dollar. It is rare to see this coin. Each half-dollar has a value of 50¢. When you add these to other coins, you count by 50s!

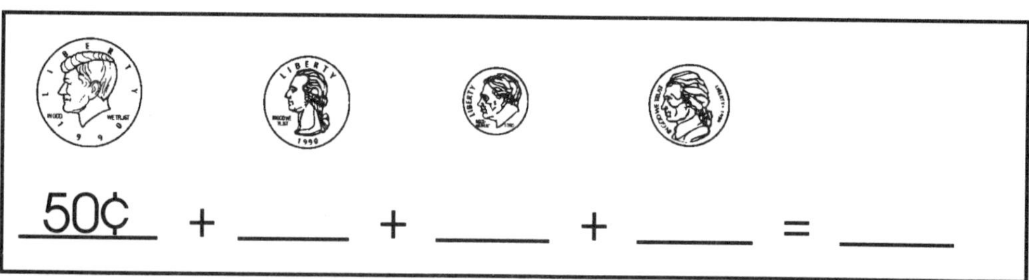

Write the total value of each group of coins.

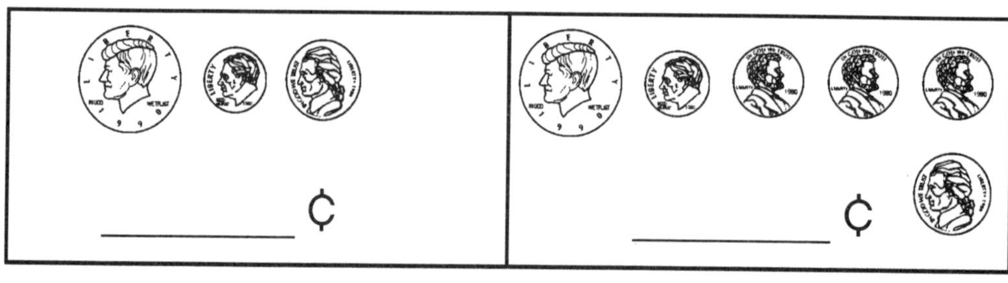

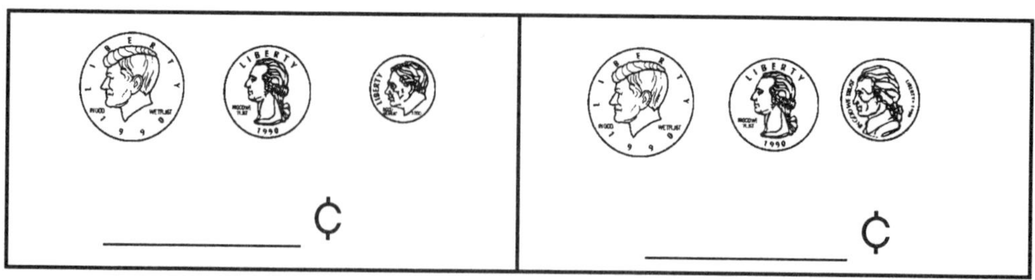

Name ______________________

Money Matters

Circle the correct answers.

1. Monica has a half-dollar.
   She needs 75¢ to buy some beads.
   What should she do?

   Add 25¢ **Subtract 25¢**

2. There are two half-dollars in Chung's piggy bank. She needs a total of 95¢ to buy a card. Does she have enough? **yes** **no**

   If yes, what will her change be? __________

3. Sam has a half-dollar in his pocket.
   He needs two quarters.
   Can he make an even trade?

   yes **no**

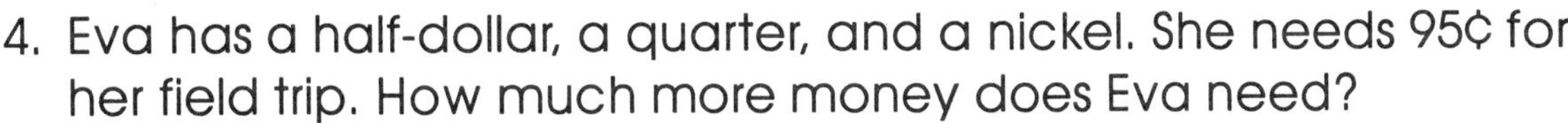

4. Eva has a half-dollar, a quarter, and a nickel. She needs 95¢ for her field trip. How much more money does Eva need?

   10¢ **15¢** **20¢**

5. Chiggles loves rawhide bones! They cost 75¢. David has two half-dollars. If David buys one bone, what will his change be?

   10¢ **15¢** **25¢**

6. If Alesha has three half-dollars, can she buy a pin that costs 80¢?

   yes **no**

Name ______________________

Meet the Dollar

Do you know what a dollar looks like? A real dollar bill has different words on it, but it looks like this:

One dollar equals 100 cents. **1 dollar = 100¢**

= **$1.00**

We usually write "one dollar" with a dollar sign.

Can you make the dollar sign? Practice!

$ $ ______________________________________

Here's what "$1.00" means:

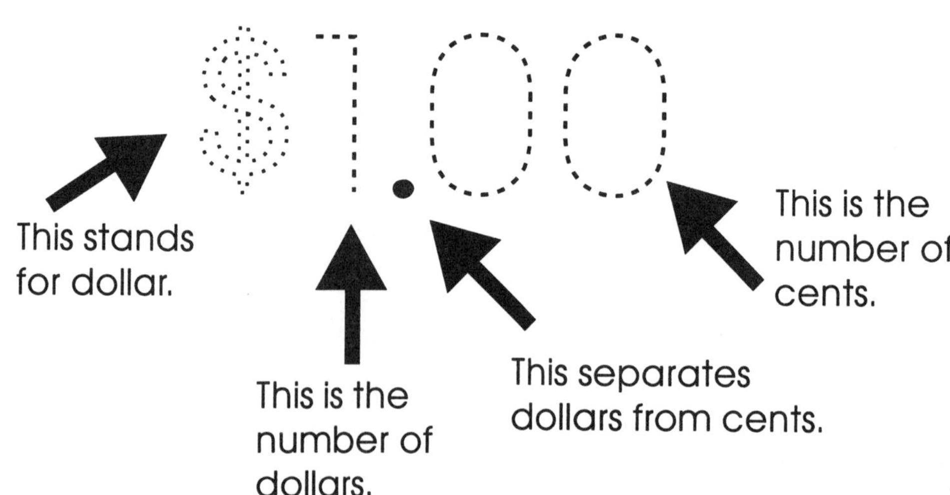

Name ______________________________

Lemonade Money

Here's the money Sam and Anna May made selling lemonade. Circle each group of change that equals one dollar. Color a dollar bill for each group circled.

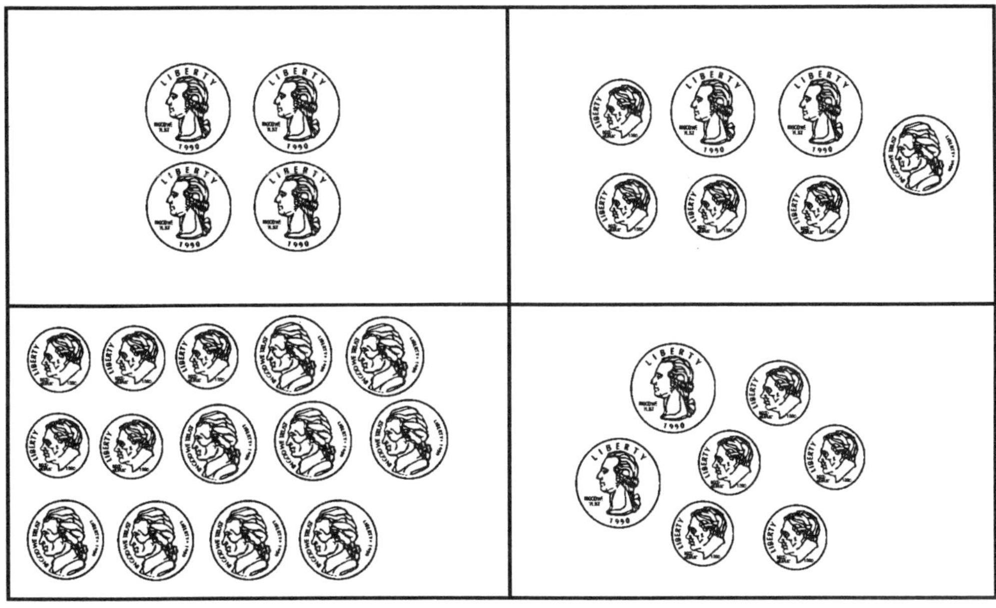

Name ______________________

Let's Write It Down

You remember that one dollar can also be written as $1.00.

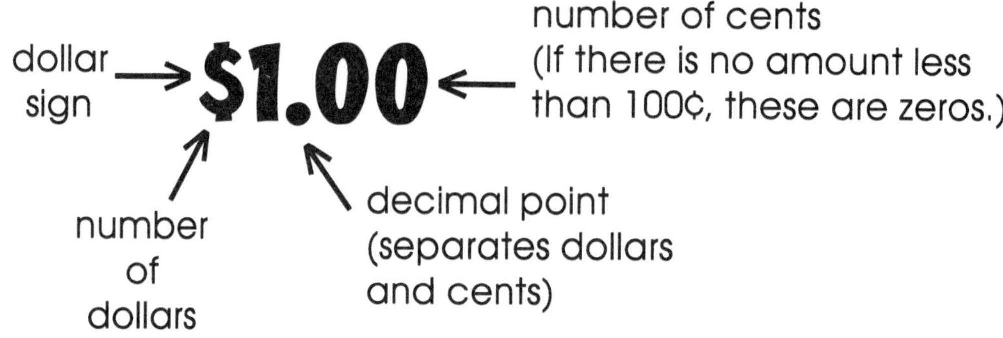

This is the most common way to write "one dollar."

Written this way, the number of dollars stay to the left of the decimal point, and the cents stay to the right!

Add the dollars, then the cents, and write the amounts.

Name ____________________

It's a Match

Here's a matching challenge! On the lines below, write down the two different ways each value can be shown. Use the Bank at the bottom of the page to help you.

_______ _______

_______ _______

_______ _______

_______ _______

_______ _______

_______ _______

Can you match these bigger bills to their amounts?

_______ _______

_______ _______

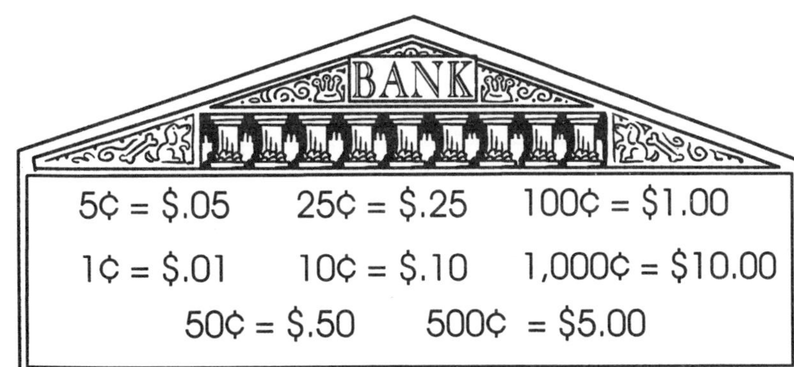

5¢ = $.05 25¢ = $.25 100¢ = $1.00

1¢ = $.01 10¢ = $.10 1,000¢ = $10.00

50¢ = $.50 500¢ = $5.00

Name ____________________

Dollar Bills and Change

$1.35

These numbers stand for a dollar bill and change.

Here's what it looks like in actual dollars and coins:

.  

Try writing these amounts.

.  = $ ____ . ____

.    = $ ____ . ____

.  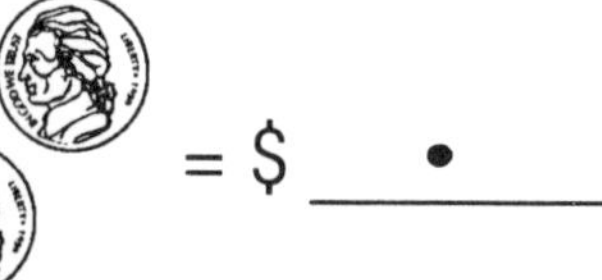 = $ ____ . ____

.   = $ ____ . ____

Name ______________________

Kids and Cash

1. David has:

•

= $ ____•____

2. Alesha has:

•

= $ ____•____

3. Mark has:

•

= $ ____•____

4. Eva has:

•

= $ ____•____

Name ______________________

Big Bills

Add the dollar bills and coins. Circle the correct total: $5.00 or $10.00.

$5.00 **$10.00**	**$5.00** **$10.00**
$5.00 **$10.00**	**$5.00** **$10.00**

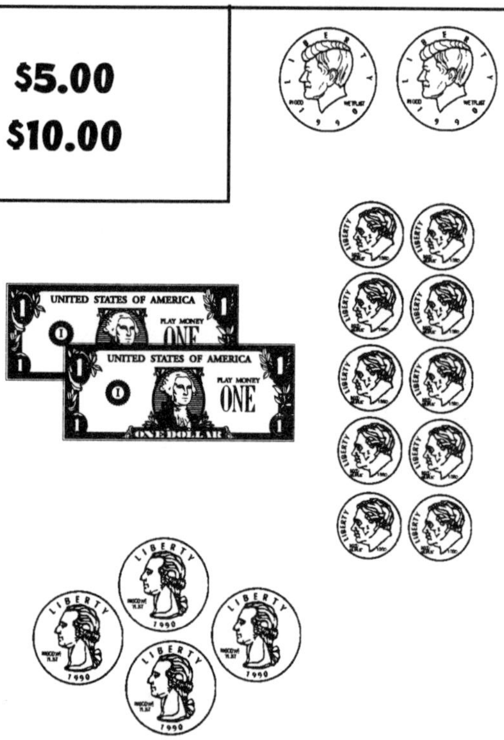

Name ____________________

Dollar Power

Adding dollars isn't any different than adding cents—but all the adding goes on in the dollar columns when there are no cents left over.

Here's an example.

$$\begin{array}{r} \$1.00 \\ +\ 5.00 \\ \hline \$\ 6.00 \end{array}$$

The total is in dollars only.

No cents means zeros in both cents columns.

Add these amounts. Regroup if you need to.

$$\begin{array}{r} \$10.00 \\ +\ \ 1.00 \\ \hline \$ \end{array} \qquad \begin{array}{r} \$\ 5.00 \\ +\ \ 7.00 \\ \hline \end{array} \qquad \begin{array}{r} \$\ 3.00 \\ +\ 9.00 \\ \hline \end{array}$$

$$\begin{array}{r} \$20.00 \\ +\ 13.00 \\ \hline \end{array} \qquad \begin{array}{r} \$\ 9.00 \\ +\ 11.00 \\ \hline \end{array} \qquad \begin{array}{r} \$14.00 \\ +\ \ 6.00 \\ \hline \end{array}$$

$$\begin{array}{r} \$\ 7.00 \\ +\ \ 6.00 \\ \hline \end{array} \qquad \begin{array}{r} \$\ 9.00 \\ +\ 13.00 \\ \hline \end{array} \qquad \begin{array}{r} \$16.00 \\ +\ \ 8.00 \\ \hline \end{array}$$

Name ____________________

Add Like the Bankers!

It's simple to add dollars when there are zeros in the cents column. It's not that much harder to add dollars and cents on paper.

```
  $4.34
+  2.25
  -----
  $  .   ← (See how we place the dollar sign
  ↑         and decimal point in the sum
            before we begin.)
```

Begin adding now, starting from the ones column, just like always.

```
      1
  $3.56
+  2.45
  -----
  $ . 1
```

When you get to the tens column and need to regroup, go ahead! Cross over the decimal, and regroup as you normally do.

```
   1←1
  $3.56
+  2.45
  -----
  $6.01
```

Add:

$3.57	$0.97	$2.51	$3.77	$4.83
+ 1.26	+ 1.89	+ 3.98	+ 3.36	+ 2.91
$	$	$	$	$

Name ____________________

Adding It Up

Add:

1. \$4.38 + 2.27	**2.** \$2.42 + 5.64	**3.** \$5.30 + 7.28
4. \$1.16 + 8.47	**5.** \$23.45 + 43.26	**6.** \$12.51 + 23.64
7. \$45.21 + 12.39	**8.** \$71.12 + 12.93	**9.** \$0.45 0.23 + 1.12
10. \$0.42 3.21 + 0.53	**11.** \$0.17 1.12 + 0.14	**12.** \$1.00 0.30 + 0.02
13. \$0.37 1.21 + 0.21	**14.** \$1.19 1.20 + 0.87	**15.** \$0.59 0.63 + 1.00

Name ____________________

Buying Power!

Sometimes we don't have enough money to buy something. Then we have to save more!

Count the money. Then subtract it from the prices. The difference shows how much **more** money is needed.

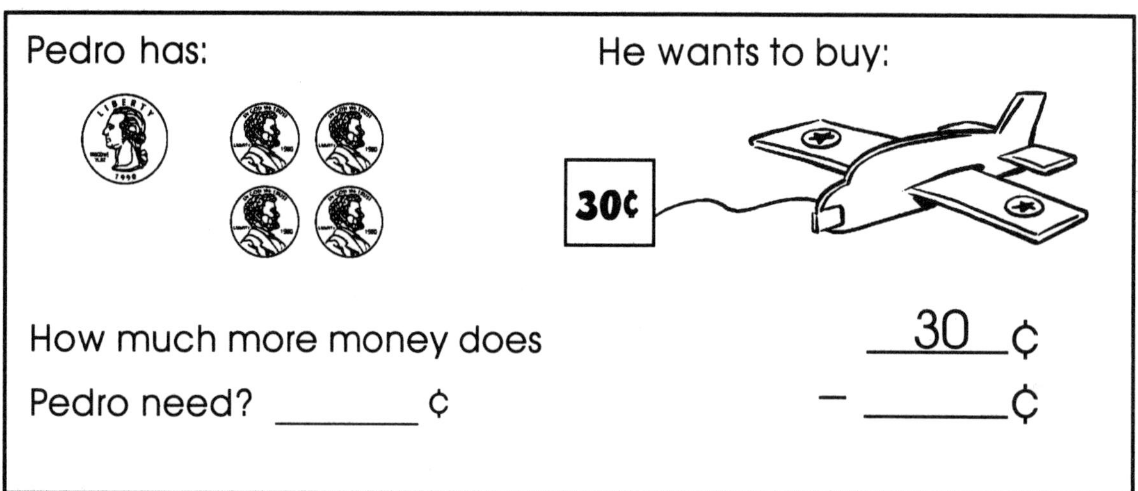
Pedro has:
He wants to buy:
30¢
How much more money does
Pedro need? ______ ¢
30 ¢
– ______ ¢

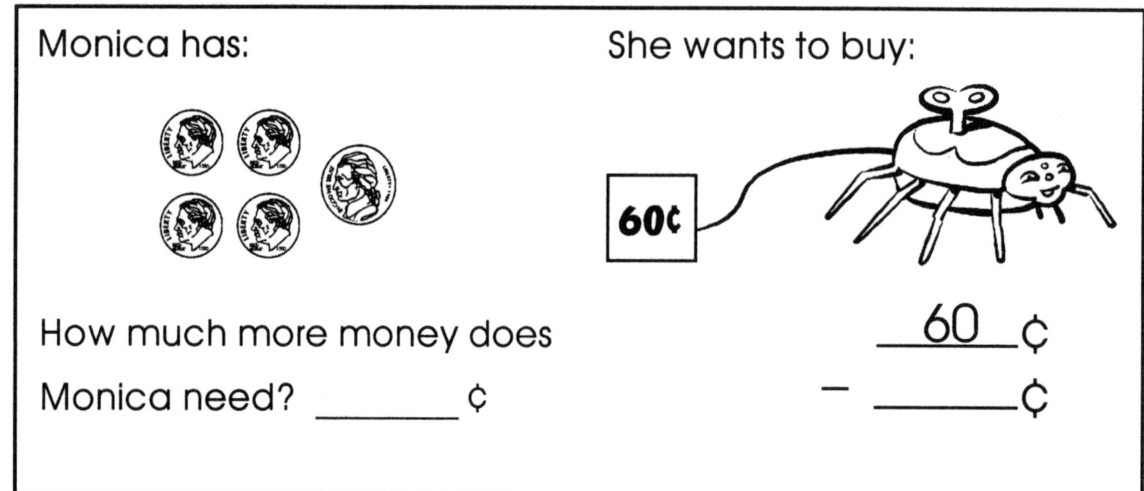
Monica has:
She wants to buy:
60¢
How much more money does
Monica need? ______ ¢
60 ¢
– ______ ¢

Name ______________________

Treat Time

Add up each group of coins. Write down the treat each person has exactly the right money to buy.

Anna May has: _______ ¢ She can buy a _________________	**Pear 45¢**	Anna May would need **10¢** more to buy the _____________ .
Eva has: _______ ¢ She can buy a _________________	**Plum 50¢**	If Eva had a nickel less, she could still buy a ___________ .
Arthur has: _______ ¢ He can buy a _________________	**Banana 35¢**	Arthur would need **5¢** more to buy the _____________ .

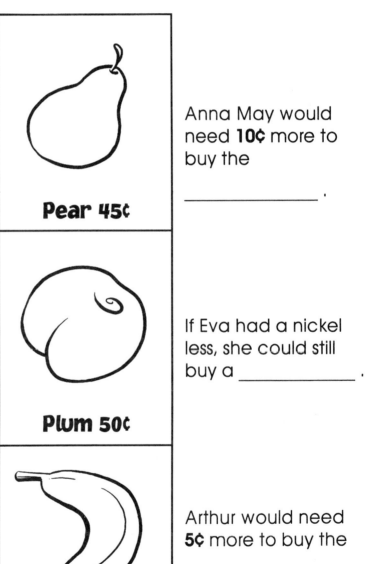

Name ______________________

Earning Money to Spend

Chung wants to buy her grandmother a special birthday present. She's been saving money for months! Help her add it up. **Hint:** You can carry over between dollars and cents, just like regular addition!

She started out with 3 quarters, or $0.75.

She earned $1.00 raking leaves.

$0.75
+$1.00
$

She traded in soda pop cans for 20¢.

+$0.20
$

Chung walked Mrs. Ross's dog for 50¢.

+$0.50
$

She made $2.00 selling lemonade.

+$2.00
$

Chung found another quarter under her bed!

+$0.25
$

Chung wants to buy a red, flowered scarf for $6.00.

Does she have enough money yet? Circle your answer.

Yes **No**

Name ______________________

David wants to buy a new leash for his dog Chiggles. The leash costs $5.00. Add David's money.

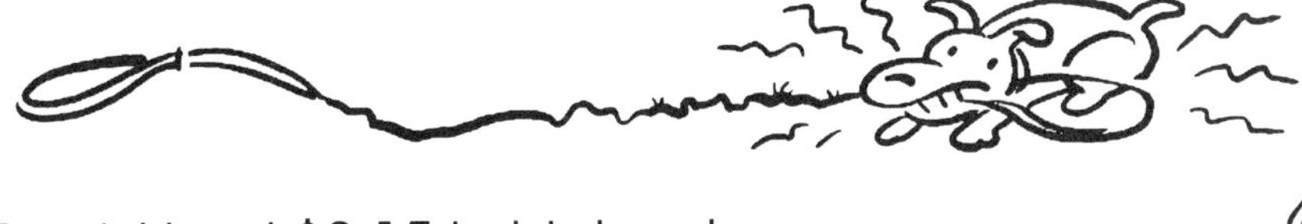

David had $2.15 in his bank. He was paid $1.00 for watering the garden.

$$\begin{array}{r} \$\,2.15 \\ +\ \$1.00 \\ \hline \$ \end{array}$$

David's father paid him $2.00 for weeding.

$$\begin{array}{r} +\$2.00 \\ \hline \$ \end{array}$$

He found a dime in the grass!

$$\begin{array}{r} +\$0.10 \\ \hline \$ \end{array}$$

Then David earned 50¢ for washing all the dishes.

$$\begin{array}{r} +\$0.50 \\ \hline \$ \end{array}$$

Can David buy the leash? **Yes** **No**

When David went to the pet store, he saw a nice rawhide bone for 50¢. He would like to buy that and the leash.

David's money = ________

Leash = –$5.00

Money left over = ________

Can David buy the bone for Chiggles, too?

Yes **No**

Name ______________________

Double Your Money!

Joel wants to buy a new game for his computer. His grandmother says she will double any money that Joel earns.

Count the money Joel earns. Then write the amount doubled.

Joel's Jobs	Money Earned	Doubled
On Saturday, he cleaned the hall closet.	$ ___ . ___	$ ___ . ___
On Monday, he helped wash Mom's car.	$ ___ . ___	$ ___ . ___
On Tuesday, he couldn't find a job, but he found this on the sidewalk.	$ ___ . ___	$ ___ . ___
On Wednesday, Joel sold one of his baseball cards.	$ ___ . ___	$ ___ . ___

Name ______________________

Count the money Joel earns.
Then write the amount doubled.

Joel's Jobs	Money Earned	Doubled
On Thursday, Joel took his aunt's dog for a walk.	$ ___ . ___	$ ___ . ___
On Friday, he helped Dad bake bread.	$ ___ . ___	$ ___ . ___
On Saturday, Joel cut the grass and watered the flowers.	$ ___ . ___	$ ___ . ___

Name ______________________

Let's "Tug" Some Sums!

Let's trade. Circle the coins on the right that equal $1.00.

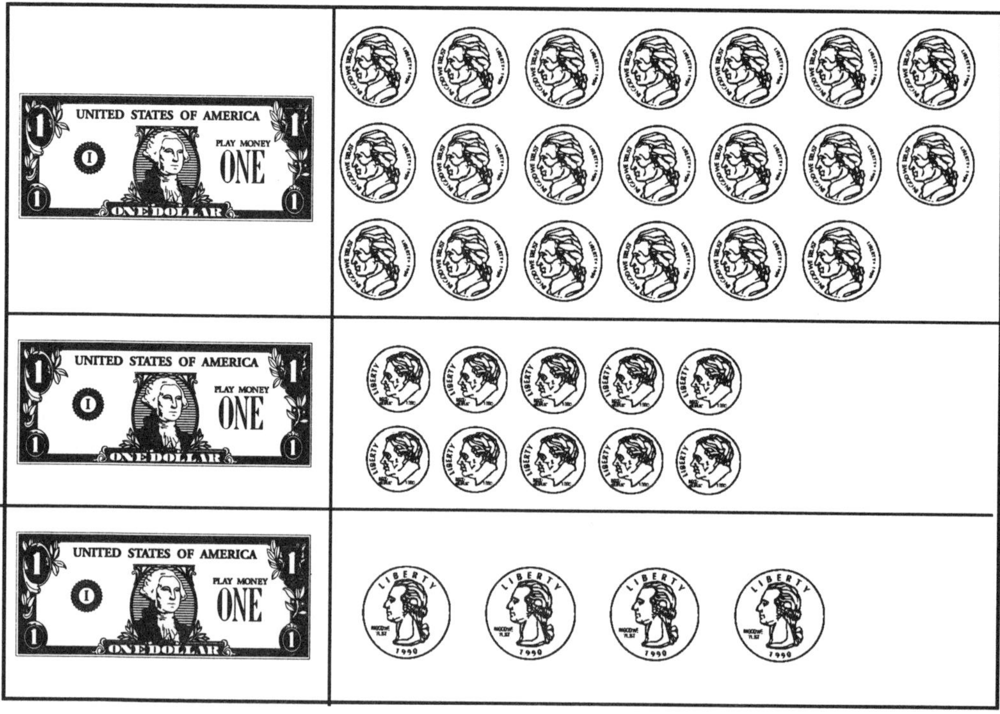

Add the coins on the barge. Then write how many dollar bills this tugboat can trade for when it docks!

This tug can trade its coins for ______ dollar(s).

Name ______________________________

Draw a line on the wave "paths" to match each tugboat to the barge with the same value.

$1.00

$5.00

$10.00

Name ______________________

Let's Make Change!

When you buy things, sometimes you have money left over. The money that you get back is called "change."

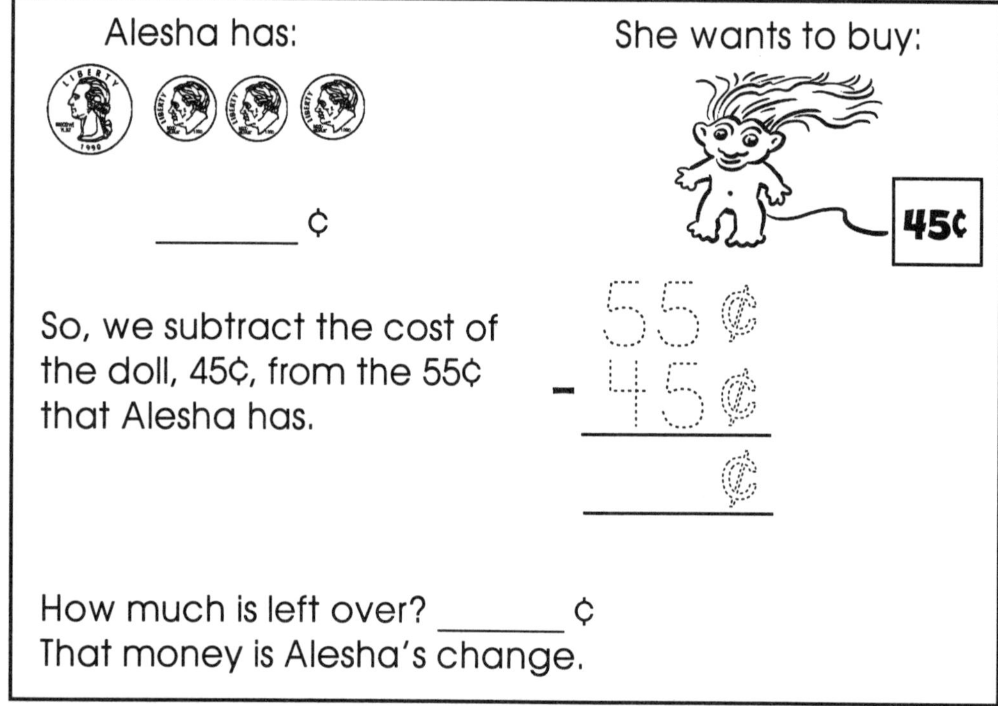

Alesha has: She wants to buy:

45¢

_______ ¢

So, we subtract the cost of the doll, 45¢, from the 55¢ that Alesha has.

55¢
− 45¢
______
¢

How much is left over? _______ ¢
That money is Alesha's change.

Let's try another!

Sam has: He wants to buy:

65¢

_______ ¢

How much change will Sam get back? _______ ¢

_______ ¢
− _______ ¢
_______ ¢

Name ______________________

Here are some more change challenges! Use subtraction to find the answers.

David has:
He wants to buy:
46¢
How much change will David get back? ________ ¢
________ ¢
– ________ ¢
________ ¢

Chung has:
She wants to buy:
55¢
How much change will Chung get back? ________ ¢
________ ¢
– ________ ¢
________ ¢

With the change Chung has, which of these treats could she buy?

35¢

20¢

25¢

Name ____________________

Changing Change

When we buy something, we are often given change back. To figure out change, we subtract.

Example:

Lindsey wants to buy a puzzle that costs $1.75.
She gives the cashier $2.00.
Should she get any money back?
Of course! It's her <u>change</u>.

Here's how it looks as a math problem.

$$\begin{array}{r} \$2.00 \\ -1.75 \\ \hline \$0.25 \end{array}$$

She gets back $0.25.

What will the cashier most likely give her in change?

one quarter   2 dimes   3 dimes

Martha went to the pet store to buy food for her hamster. It cost $4.25. Martha gave the cashier a five-dollar bill.

$$\begin{array}{r} \$5.00 \\ -4.25 \\ \hline \end{array}$$

Let's figure the change. What coins will she get back?

Circle any coin combinations she might be given. You will have more than one answer.

A. 2 quarters and 1dime
B. 7 dimes and 1 nickel
C. 2 quarters, 2 dimes, and 1 nickel
D. 1 half-dollar and 1 quarter
E. 3 quarters

Name ________________________

Change Champs

Have each shopper choose the most expensive toy each one can buy. Then help them figure out their change. Write each shopper's name under the right toy.

Maria has $5.00.	Tony has $2.00.
Jonathan has $1.00.	Janesa has $9.00
David has $10.00.	Eva has $6.00.

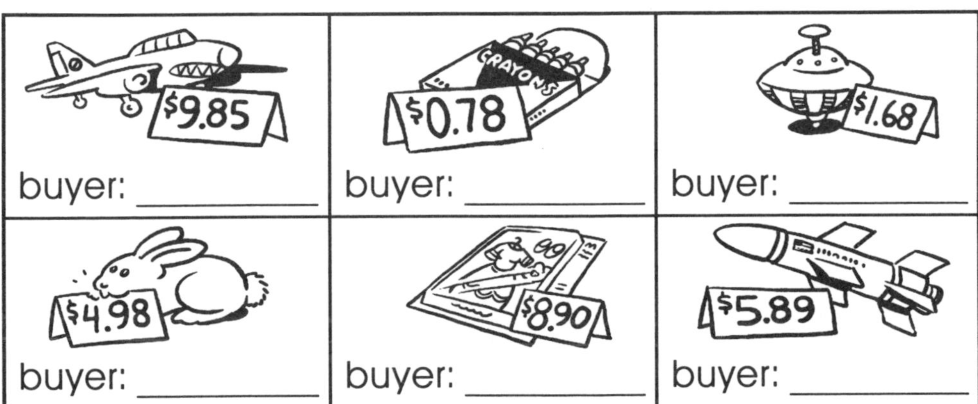

Maria:
$5.00
− ______

Tony:
$2.00
− ______

David:
$10.00
− ______

Janesa:
$9.00
− ______

Jonathan:
$1.00
− ______

Eva:
$6.00
− ______

Name ___________________________

Change Challenges

Time to go shopping. Help each student compute his or her change.

Let's figure the change for Martha's sunglasses.

1. Martha picks out some sunglasses.
   The price is $9.40.
   She hands the cashier a $10.00 bill.

$$\begin{array}{r} \$10.00 \\ -\ \ 9.40 \\ \hline \$ \end{array}$$

   Now let's decide what the change should be!
   Circle the correct coins:

2. Maria picks out a stuffed tiger that costs $4.28.
   She hands the cashier $4.50.

$$\begin{array}{r} \$\ 4.50 \\ -\ 4.28 \\ \hline \$ \end{array}$$

   Circle the correct change.

Name ______________________

3. Alex sees a football for $2.45. He hands the cashier three dollars.

$ 3.00
– ______
$

Circle the correct change.

4. Alesha loves the postcard with the funny dog on the front! The price is 84¢. She hands the cashier one dollar.

$ 1.00
– ______
$

Circle the correct change.

5. Mark finds a piggy bank at a garage sale. The price is $1.25. Mark pays with two dollars.

$ 2.00
– ______
$

Circle the correct change.

Name ______________________

Saving Is Adding

When you save money, it adds up! That is because each time you save a new amount, you add that to what you had before. Let's try a few story problems.

1. Mark had $3.49 in his piggy bank. He made $1.00 shoveling snow. How much did he have then?

   Mark's grandmother sent him $5.00 for his birthday. How much did he have in savings then? ____________

$3.49
+ ______
$

+ 5.00
$

$9.49
+ ______
$

2. Eva is saving money for a trip. So far, she has $9.49. If she earns $2.00 at the craft fair, $1.50 for raking leaves, and 75¢ for washing out her kitten's water bowl, how much has Eva saved?

   ____

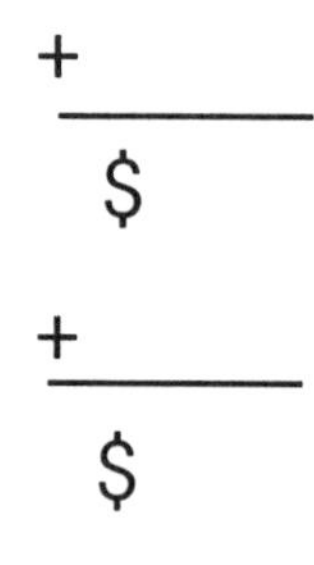

+ ______
$

+ ______
$

Name ______________________

3. Maria had $6.27 saved in her bank. Maria's father gave her $4.00 for helping him clean the garage. While they were cleaning, Maria found a half-dollar. Her father said she could keep it. How much has Maria saved?

    $ 6.27
    + ______
    $
    + ______
    $

____

4. David keeps his savings all over his room! He has $1.67 in his bank, $2.10 in a little box, and 75¢ in his wallet. How much has David saved?

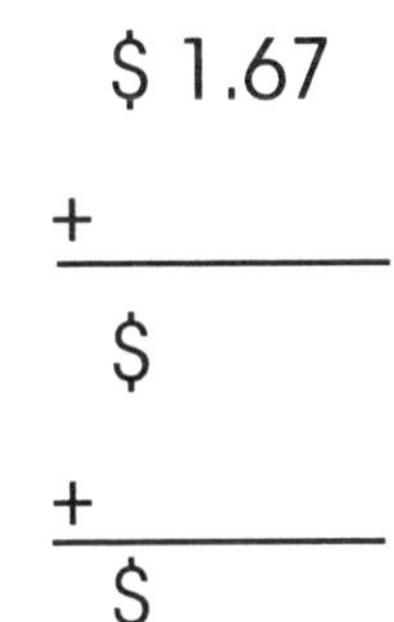

    $ 1.67
    + ______
    $
    + ______
    $

____

5. If David gets $2.00 in a birthday card, how much money will he have then? ______________

Name ______________________

Spending Is Subtracting

When you spend money, you are always subtracting. That's because you are taking away money from your savings. Here's an example.

1. Alesha saved \$3.75. Then she decided to buy a pen set for \$1.95.

   $3.75
   –$1.95
   $

   How much did Alesha have left in her savings? ________

   Now she buys ice cream for 85¢.

   – $0.85
   $

   How much does she have left now? ___________

2. Joel gets \$2.00 a week for allowance. He decides to buy a toy car for \$1.79. How much will he have left over?

   $2.00
   –$1.79
   $

   ____

3. If Joel waits until his next allowance day, and then wants to buy a comic book for \$2.25, will he be able to do it?

   yes **no**

Name ____________________

4. Chung has saved $2.00.
   If she buys a card for 95¢,
   how much will she have left?

   ____

$2.00
–$ ______
$

5. Andrea has saved $5.00.
   She wants to take a bottle
   of bubbles with her on the
   class picnic. The bubbles
   cost $2.95. How much
   will she have left over?

   ____

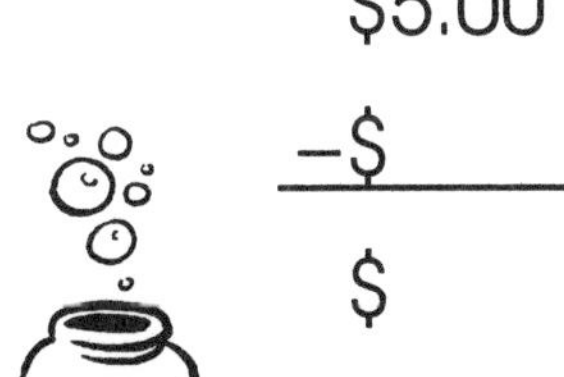

$5.00
–$ ______
$

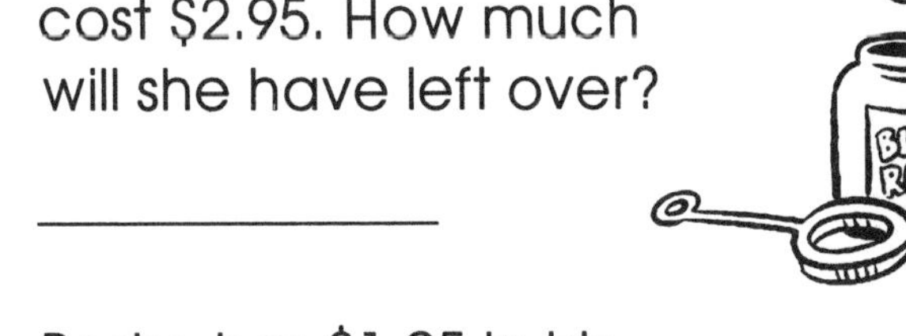
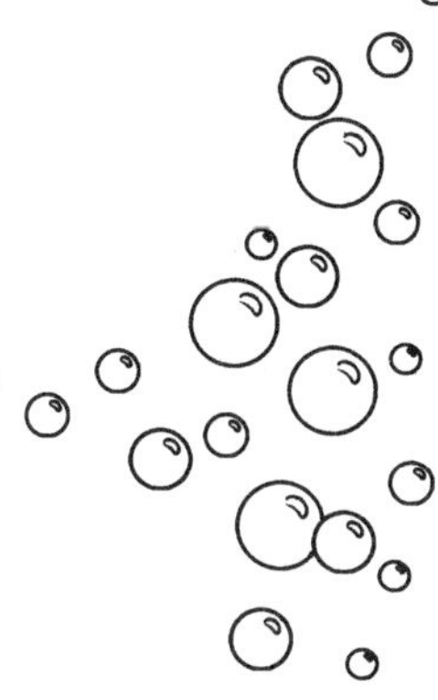

6. Pedro has $1.95 in his
   wallet. He decides to buy
   an apple for a snack. It's
   79¢. How much will he
   have left over?

   ____

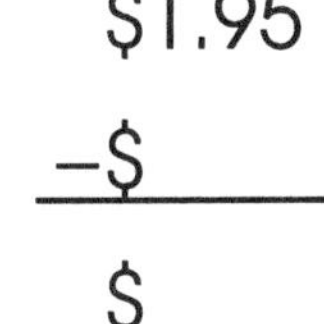

$1.95
–$ ______
$

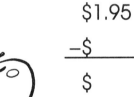

7. Here is all the money Eva
   brought back from her trip.
   Circle the toy she can buy.

Name ____________________

Subtraction Detectives

Here's a fun challenge! Let's find out what each third-grader bought. The table shows how much money each student had to spend.

David	$20.00
Samantha	$20.00
Steven	$20.00
Christina	$10.00
Mark	$10.00
Andrea	$10.00

Your only clue is how much change each student had after his or her purchase!

Here are the items that David, Samantha, and Steven bought. When you figure out who bought what, write each name in the box underneath the correct item.

$15.50	$19.75	$8.75

David	Samantha	Steven
$20.00	$ 20.00	$ 20.00
–	–	–
$11.25	$ 4.50	$ 0.25

Name ______________________

Here are the items that Christina, Mark, and Andrea bought. When you figure out who bought what, write each name in the box underneath the correct item.

$9.90	$7.50	$5.00

Christina	Mark	Andrea
$ 10.00	$ 10.00	$ 10.00
−	−	−
$2.50	$ 5.00	$ 0.10

Of the six students:

1. Who spent the least money? ______________

2. Who spent the most money? ______________

3. Who got back the smallest amount of change?

   ____

4. Who got back the largest amount of change?

   ____

5. What would you have bought from the items shown?

   ____

6. Who bought your favorite item? ______________

Name ______________________

Spending and Saving

As we save and spend money, we have to add <u>and</u> subtract all the time. This is so we can keep track of how much money we have.

Add and subtract to find the answers.

1. Monica saved \$2.50. Then she earned another \$1.25. Monica was invited to Maria's birthday party. She spent \$3.00 on Maria's gift. What does she have left over?

   ____

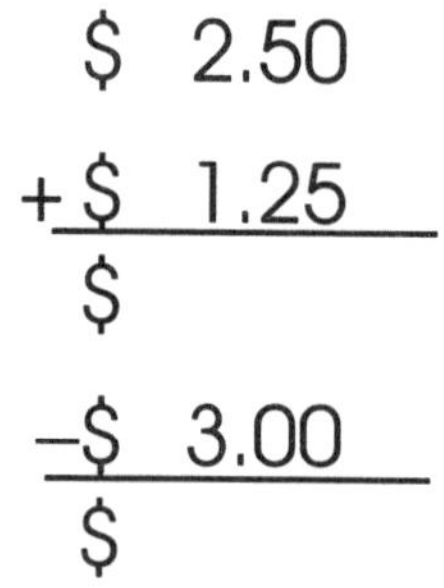

$$\begin{array}{r} \$\ 2.50 \\ +\$\ 1.25 \\ \hline \$ \\ -\$\ 3.00 \\ \hline \$ \end{array}$$

2. David got \$5.00 for his birthday. On a field trip, he spent \$3.95 for a model of a plane. Then he earned \$1.00 by helping his aunt in her yard. How much money does David have now? ____________

$$\begin{array}{r} \$\ 5.00 \\ -\$\ 3.95 \\ \hline \$ \\ +\$\ 1.00 \\ \hline \$ \end{array}$$

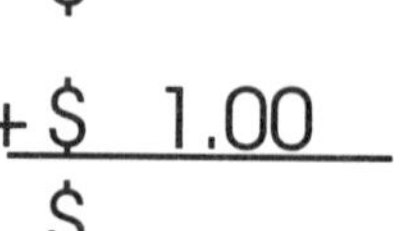

3. Jason's uncle gave him \$3.00 as a gift. Jason had saved \$10.00. He decided to buy a paint set for \$12.95. How much does Jason have left?

   ____

$$\begin{array}{r} \$\ 3.00 \\ +\$\ 10.00 \\ \hline \$ \\ -\$\ 12.95 \\ \hline \$ \end{array}$$

Name ______________________

4. Alesha had $12.00. She decided to buy little stuffed animals. She bought a bear for $5.00, a rabbit for $3.50, and a kitten for $2.95. How much money does she have left? __________

$ 12.00
– $ 5.00
$
– $ 3.50
$
– $ 2.95
$

5. Joel wants to buy a magic kit for $10.95. He saves $15.00. At the store, he also sees a juggling set for $3.65. How much money does Joel have left after his purchases? __________

$ 15.00
– $ 10.95
$
– $ 3.65
$

6. Eva has saved $5.75. She wants to buy three goldfish for $3.15. At the pet store, the owner says she should also buy a snail for 65¢. How much money will Eva have left over? __________

$ 5.75
– $ 3.15
$
– $ .65
$

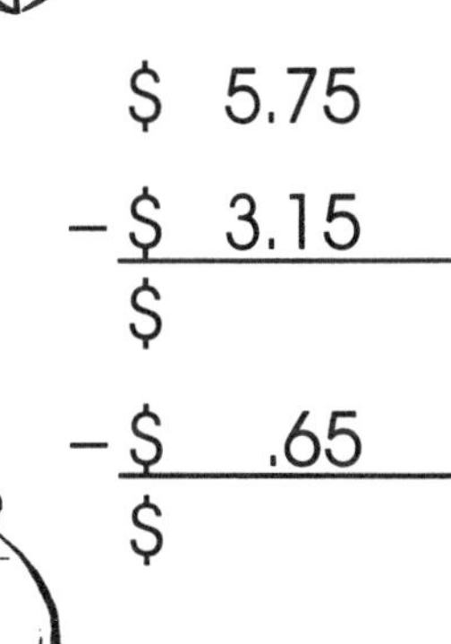

Name ________________________

Up and Down

Larger amounts of money are made of paper.

Smaller amounts of money are made as coins.

Both can be used to trade for things of value. Find each sum. Circle the side of the teeter-totter that will fall. The side with the greater amount will go down.

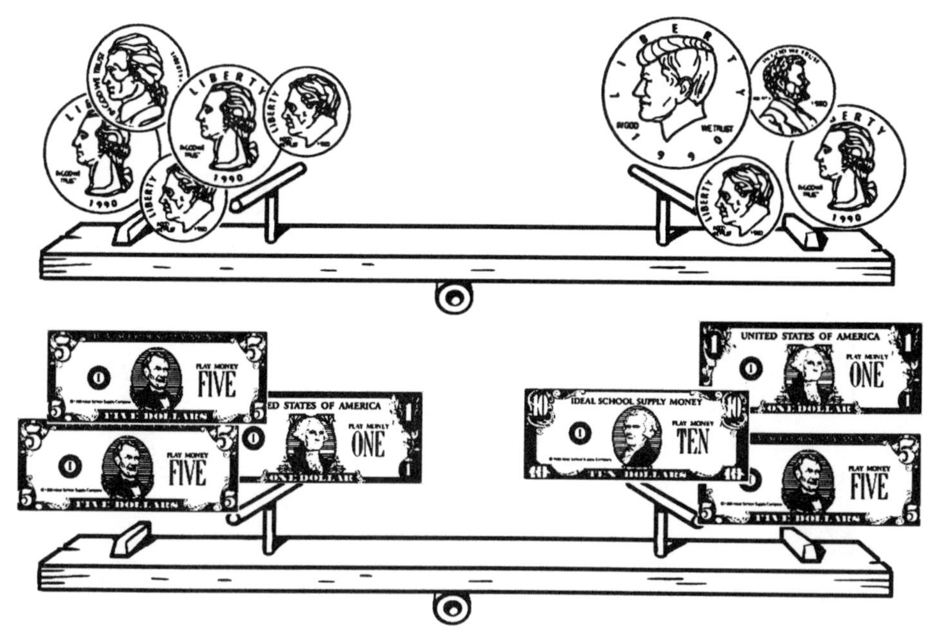

Name ______________________

Let's Compare!

Add each pair of sums. Circle the side with the greater amount.

1.  Total: $ ____ . ____	 Total: $ ____ . ____
2.  Total: $ ____ . ____	 Total: $ ____ . ____
3.  Total: $ ____ . ____	 Total: $ ____ . ____

Name ____________________

The Art of Estimation

Estimation makes it much easier to add or subtract in your head. You can estimate by rounding numbers out to the nearest tens place. Numbers below 5 should be rounded down, and numbers of 5 and above should be rounded up. Example: Round 26¢ to 30¢.

These are on sale today in the lunchroom.

You have this money:

You want the pizza.

Round or estimate the cost. ______ ¢

Do you have enough money? **Yes** **No**

The banana and the cookie look good!

Add the estimated prices. ________ + ________ = ________

Do you have enough money?

Yes **No**

Name ______________________

Line Up for Lunch

David has this money:

He has ______ cents.

He wants to buy milk and a banana to go with his sandwich from home.

If he buys milk , will he have enough left to buy the banana ?

Yes **No**

David's money = ______ ¢

Estimate the milk price − ______ ¢

He has about this much left over. ______ ¢

Eva has this money:

She wants to buy the milk and something else to eat.
Estimate to see if she has enough for milk and pizza.

Estimate the milk price ______
Estimate the pizza price ______

Does she have enough for both?

Yes **No**

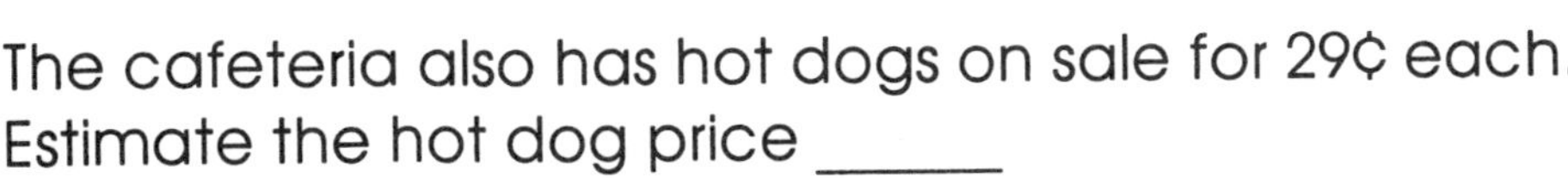

The cafeteria also has hot dogs on sale for 29¢ each.
Estimate the hot dog price ______

Can Eva buy milk and a hot dog? **Yes** **No**

Name ______________________

Let's Estimate!

Sometimes we need to make a quick guess about money. So, we estimate!

Example:

Anthony sees a little car for 88¢.
He thinks: "That's about 90¢!
I have 90¢. Good, I can buy it!"

Circle the correct answers.

1. Mark sees a pinwheel for sale.
   It costs 79¢. That's about:

   60¢ **70¢** **80¢**

   He has 91¢.
   Does he have enough?

   Yes **No**

2. Lee wants to buy a bracelet.
   It costs 68¢. That's about:

   60¢ **70¢** **80¢**

   She has 50¢.
   About how much more does Lee need?

   10¢ **20¢** **30¢** **40¢**

   If Lee's mother gave her another 50¢ and Lee bought the bracelet, would she have enough money to buy a pinwheel, too?

   Yes **No**

Name ____________________

3. Earl wants to buy a toy car.
   It costs $1.39. That's about

   $1.30 **$1.40** **$1.50**

   He has $1.75.
   Does he have enough?

   Yes **No**

4. Chung would like to buy a hot dog. It costs 57¢.
   That's about:

   60¢ **50¢** **70¢**

   She has 65¢.
   Does she have enough?

   Yes **No**

5. Eva sees a ball that she really likes. It costs $2.49.
   That's about:

   $2.00 **$2.50** **$3.00**

   She has $3.00.
   Does she have enough?

   Yes **No**

6. David wants to buy a new pen.
   It costs $2.89. That's about

   $2.00 **$2.50** **$3.00**

   He has $2.75.
   Does he have enough?

   Yes **No**

Name ______________________

Estimate Away!

When we want to know if our addition is close, we simply estimate.

If the real amounts are:	**We round to the nearest ten cents:**	
\$0.84	\$0.80	(4 or less, round down.)
–\$0.25	–\$0.30	(5 or more, round up.)
\$1.09	\$1.10	

Does our estimate look close? Yes! Then, it's probably right!

Let's try another problem!

If the real amounts are:	**We round to the nearest ten cents:**
\$0.34	\$0.30
+\$0.21	+\$0.20
\$0.55	\$

Are we close? Yes! Good! Then it's probably right!

Make a quick estimate on these problems:

1.
\$0.67 ________
+\$0.32 + ________
\$0.99

2.
\$0.52 ________
+\$0.86 + ________
\$1.38

Were you close? __________

Name ________________________

Estimate each sum. If your sum is close, star your answer. If it is not close, add the original equation again to get the correct answer.

3.

		Try again:
\$0.38	______	______
+\$0.24	+ ______	+ ______
\$0.62		

4.

		Try again:
\$0.84	______	______
+\$0.36	+ ______	+ ______
\$1.20		

5.

		Try again:
\$0.21	______	______
\$0.53	______	______
+\$0.36	+ ______	+ ______
\$1.10		

6.

		Try again:
\$0.37	______	______
\$0.52	______	______
+\$0.22	+ ______	+ ______
\$1.11		

Name ____________________________

Shopping in the Next Galaxy

Mrs. Bleepz goes to the Zotz Market for her groceries. Her children—Blurp, Zeezo, and Bleeza—go with her.

1. Mrs. Bleepz asks Bleeza to pick out the galactic juice. She says, "Find a brand that costs less than $1.00 a gallon."

   Circle the galactic juice Bleeza picks.

Starshine Berry
3 gallons/$3.00

Galaxy Grape
2 gallons/$1.95

Transport Treat
2 gallons/$2.00

2. Mrs. Bleepz sends Blurp to buy sand-snake stew, but she wants a brand that costs $1.00 a can.

   Circle Blurp's choice of stew.

Snazzy Snake
2 cans for
$3.50

Slinky Stew
2 cans for
$2.00

Can-O-Viper
2 cans for
$2.25

3. Zeezo has to find mudwort muffins that are 25¢ each.

   Circle the brand he chooses.

Wort Wonders
4 for $4.00

Mud Muffins
4 for $1.00

Best Mud
4 for $2.00

Name ______________________

4. Mrs. Bleepz tells each of her children they can each have a treat, and gives them $3.00 to divide.

   Circle a choice for each kid. The treats must add up to exactly $3.00.

Bleeza:	Grummi Snakes $0.75	Caramel Sand Beetle $1.05	Galactic Gum $0.90
Blurp:	Snake-sicle $0.90	Grape Goo $1.25	Desert Toad Treat $1.15
Zeezo:	Wortberry Tarts $0.85	ZapDrops $1.00	Plutonic Bar $1.35

5. At the checkout lane, all of Mrs. Bleepz's groceries add up to $22.85.

   She hands the cashier:   

   Calculate her change: $ ____________

   \- 22.85 ____________

6. Blurp sees a Desert Dragon comic book he wants. Can Mrs. Bleepz buy it with her change?

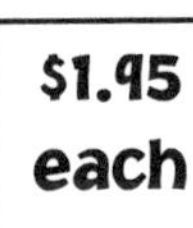

Yes **No**

Name ______________________

The Money Challenge!

Work your way down this challenging path! Earn your way to the finish line!

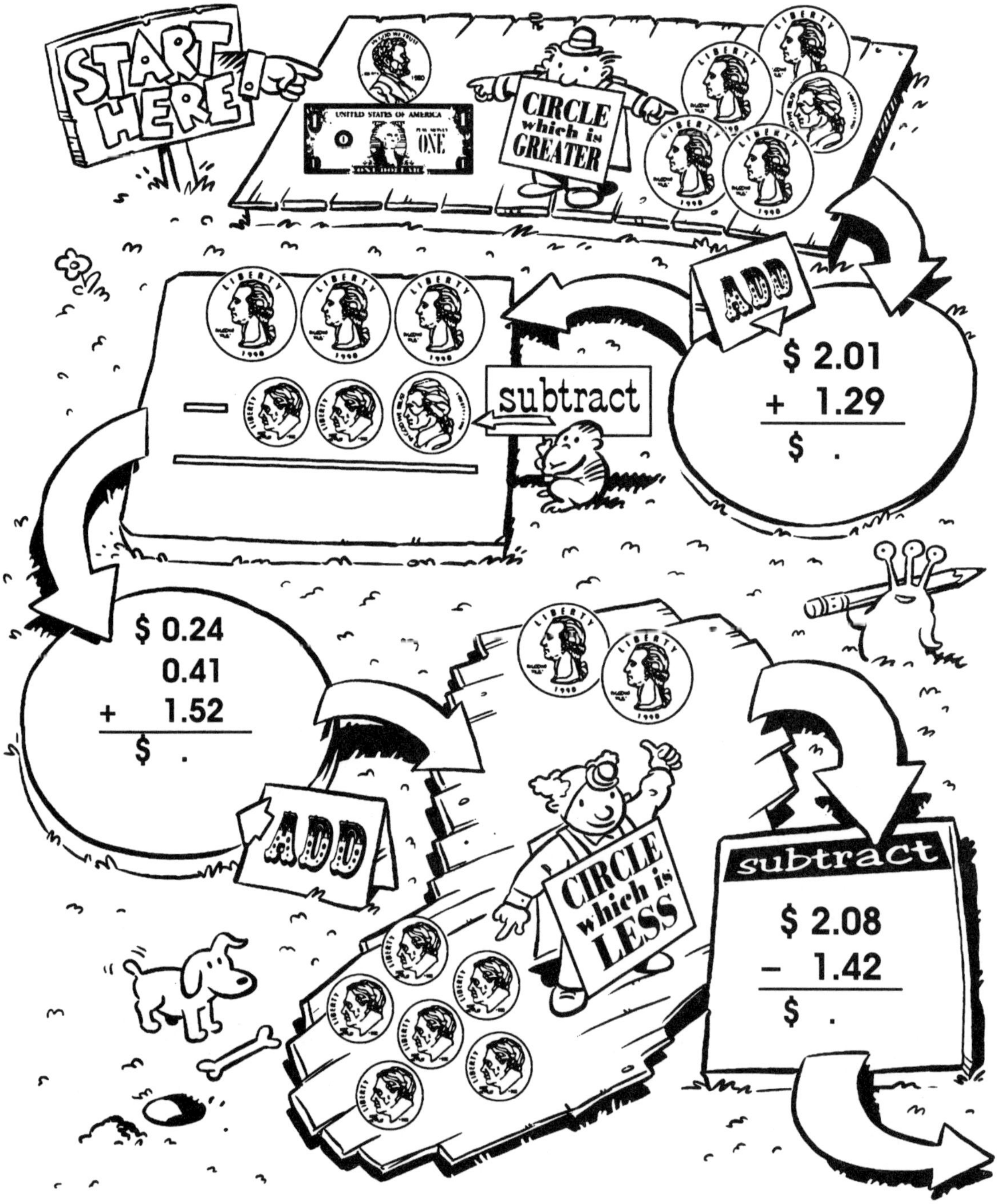

START HERE!

CIRCLE which is GREATER

ONE

ADD

$$
\begin{array}{r}
\$\ 2.01 \\
+\ \ 1.29 \\
\hline
\$\ \ \ \ .\ \ \ \
\end{array}
$$

subtract

−

$$
\begin{array}{r}
\$\ 0.24 \\
0.41 \\
+\ \ 1.52 \\
\hline
\$\ \ \ \ .\ \ \ \
\end{array}
$$

ADD

CIRCLE which is LESS

subtract

$$
\begin{array}{r}
\$\ 2.08 \\
-\ \ 1.42 \\
\hline
\$\ \ \ \ .\ \ \ \
\end{array}
$$

Name ____________________

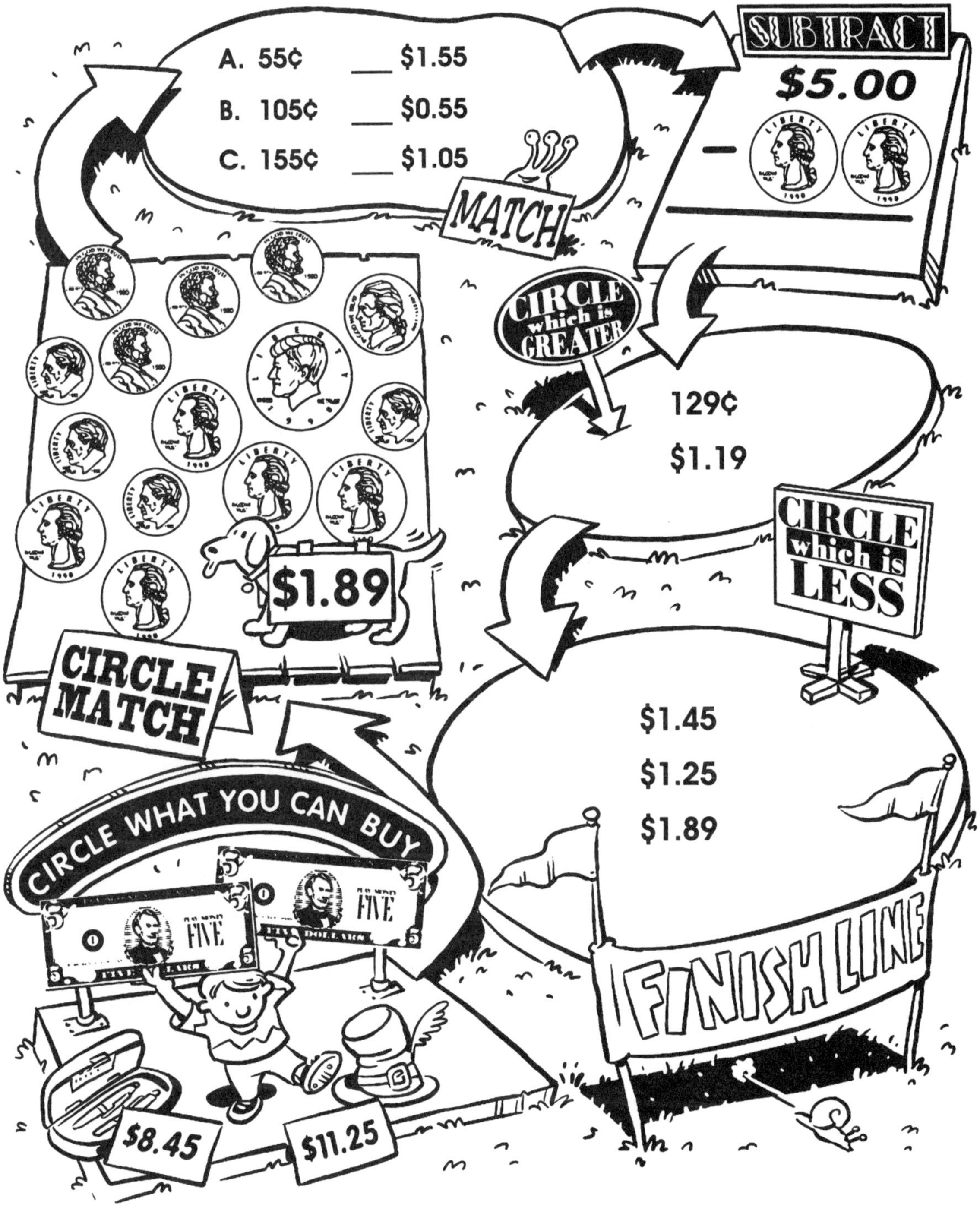

MATCH

A. 55¢ ___ $1.55

B. 105¢ ___ $0.55

C. 155¢ ___ $1.05

SUBTRACT

$5.00

−

CIRCLE which is GREATER

129¢

$1.19

CIRCLE MATCH

$1.89

CIRCLE which is LESS

$1.45

$1.25

$1.89

CIRCLE WHAT YOU CAN BUY

$8.45

$11.25

FINISH LINE

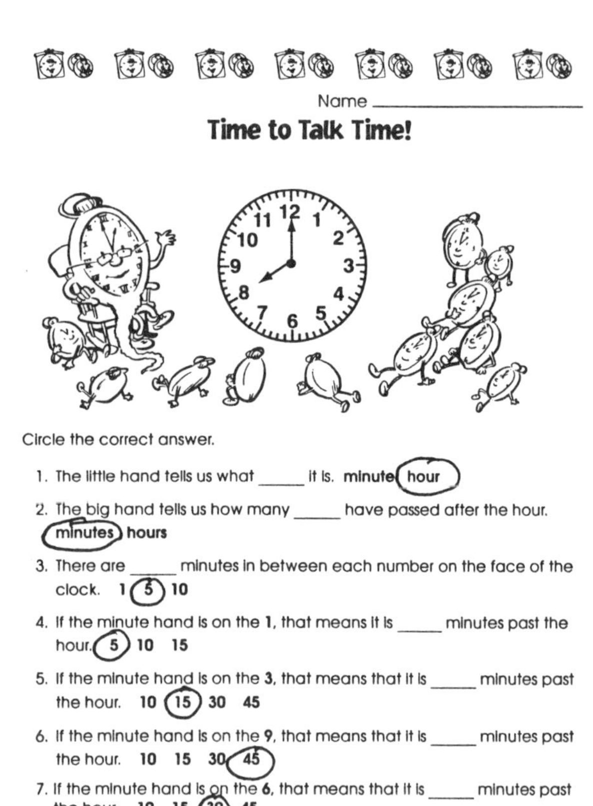

Name ______________________

Time to Talk Time!

Circle the correct answer.

1. The little hand tells us what _____ it is. minute (hour)
2. The big hand tells us how many _____ have passed after the hour. (minutes) hours
3. There are _____ minutes in between each number on the face of the clock. 1 (5) 10
4. If the minute hand is on the **1**, that means it is _____ minutes past the hour. (5) 10 15
5. If the minute hand is on the **3**, that means that it is _____ minutes past the hour. 10 (15) 30 45
6. If the minute hand is on the **9**, that means that it is _____ minutes past the hour. 10 15 30 (45)
7. If the minute hand is on the **6**, that means that it is _____ minutes past the hour. 10 15 (30) 45

Page 4

Time to Talk Time! cont.

Name ______________________

Complete the statement below. Fill in each blank with the word that matches the hour on the clock below.

Learning to tell time is very important! So, take (9:00) out your tinted (6:00), tilted (11:00), tin (4:00) timepiece, and learn to tell (2:00), time (12:00)!

Page 5

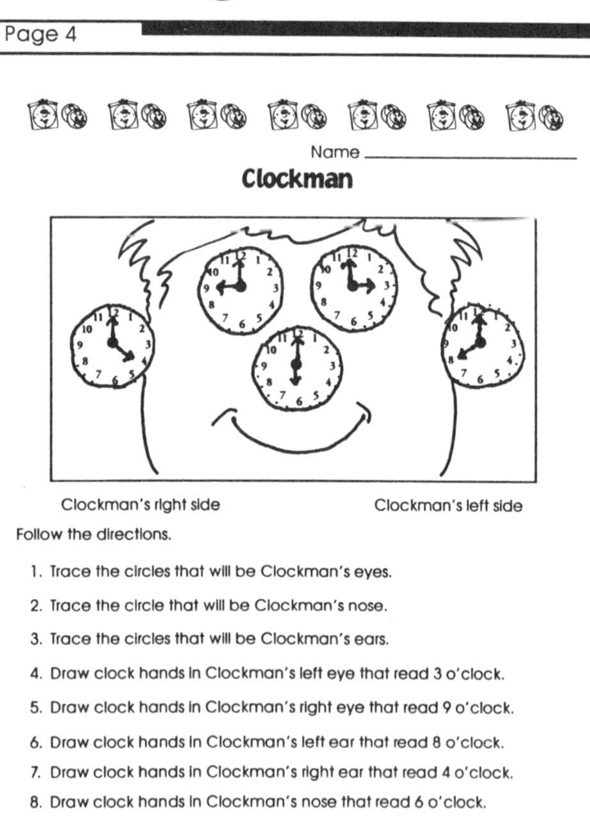

Name ______________________

Clockman

Follow the directions.

1. Trace the circles that will be Clockman's eyes.
2. Trace the circle that will be Clockman's nose.
3. Trace the circles that will be Clockman's ears.
4. Draw clock hands in Clockman's left eye that read 3 o'clock.
5. Draw clock hands in Clockman's right eye that read 9 o'clock.
6. Draw clock hands in Clockman's left ear that read 8 o'clock.
7. Draw clock hands in Clockman's right ear that read 4 o'clock.
8. Draw clock hands in Clockman's nose that read 6 o'clock.
9. Draw a big smile on Clockman's face!

Page 6

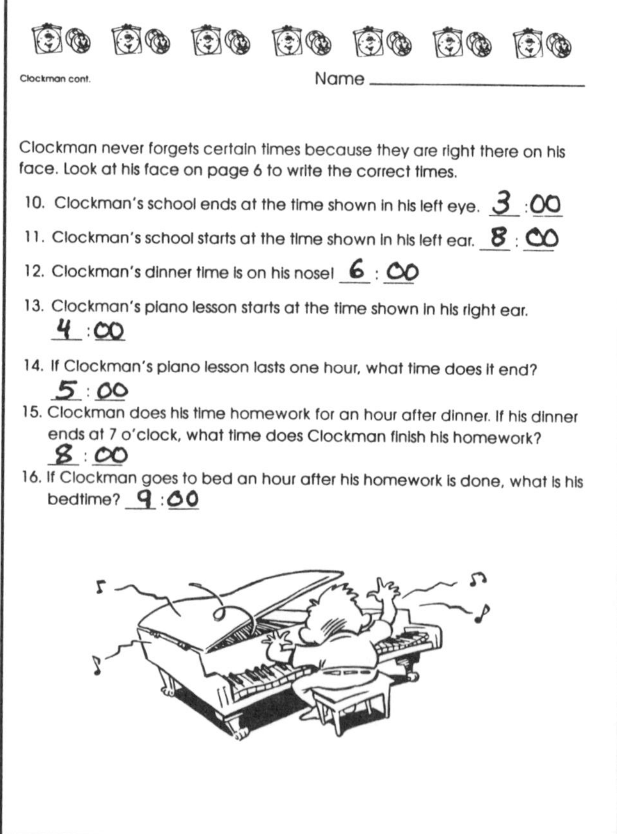

Clockman cont.

Name ______________________

Clockman never forgets certain times because they are right there on his face. Look at his face on page 6 to write the correct times.

10. Clockman's school ends at the time shown in his left eye. 3 : 00
11. Clockman's school starts at the time shown in his left ear. 8 : 00
12. Clockman's dinner time is on his nose! 6 : 00
13. Clockman's piano lesson starts at the time shown in his right ear. 4 : 00
14. If Clockman's piano lesson lasts one hour, what time does it end? 5 : 00
15. Clockman does his time homework for an hour after dinner. If his dinner ends at 7 o'clock, what time does Clockman finish his homework? 8 : 00
16. If Clockman goes to bed an hour after his homework is done, what is his bedtime? 9 : 00

Page 7

Name ____________

Halfway Around the Clock

The big hand is on the six when the time is half past the hour. If the little hand points to the 9, and the big hand is pointing to the 6, what time is it?

9 : 30

Write these times.

8 : 30

11 : 30

1 : 30

When the minute hand is halfway around the clock, that's a half-hour. A half-hour is 30 minutes long. That's why we write 5:30 for half past 5.

Write the times.

1. A half-hour past 12 o'clock is 12 : 30.
2. A half-hour past 8 o'clock is 8 : 30.
3. 6:30 is a half-hour after 6 : 00.
4. 2:30 is a half-hour past 2 : 00.
5. 5:30 is a half-hour past 5 : 00.
6. 10:30 is a half-hour past 10 : 00.
7. 2:00 is a half-hour before 2 : 30.
8. 8:00 is a half-hour before 8 : 30.

Page 8

Name ____________

The Hidden Half-Hour Puzzle

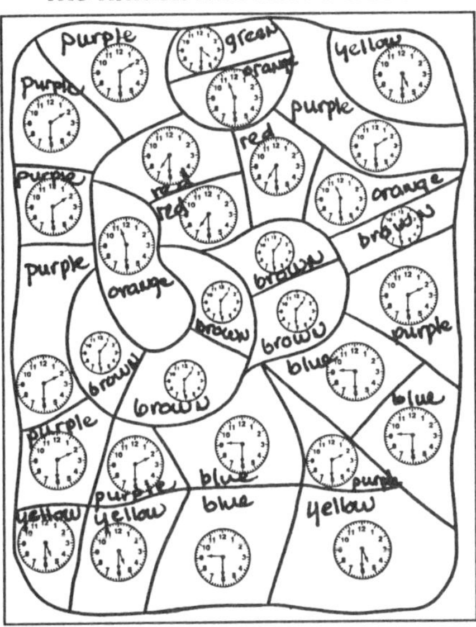

Color this puzzle using this key:

If the clock says . . .

7:30, color the shape red.

2:30, color the shape purple.

5:30, color the shape yellow.

4:30, color the shape green.

9:30, color the shape blue

11:30, color the shape orange

1:30, color the shape brown

Page 9

Name ____________

Quarters of an Hour

One-fourth of an hour is 15 minutes. Each time the minute hand moves 15 minutes, we call that a "quarter-hour."

Count by 5s to find each quarter-hour time.

The last quarter-hour is the new hour!

This is a quarter past the hour, or 12:15.

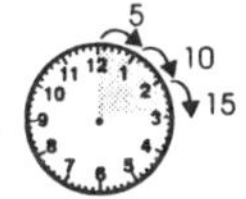

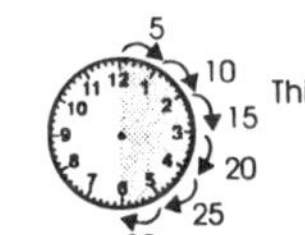

This is half past the hour, or 12:30.

This is three-quarters past the hour, or 12:45.

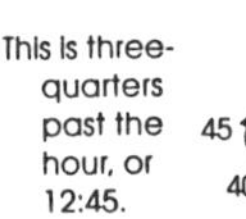

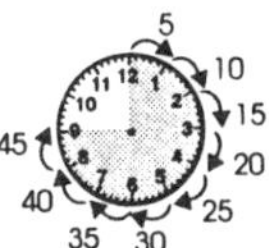

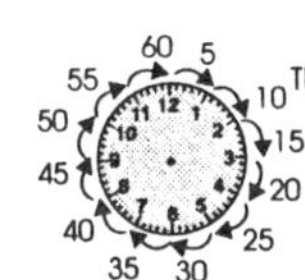

The last quarter-hour completes the hour. It is now 1 o'clock.

Place the minute hand on each clock to show the quarter-hours.

2:15

2:30

2:45

The final quarter hour would be: **2:50 3:00 3:05** (3:00 circled)

Page 10

Name ____________

Stops and Starts

1. Billy had a great time doing chalk drawings in the driveway at 2:15. It rained 15 minutes later! What time did the chalk drawings vanish?
   2:30

2. Carrie loves to rollerblade. She went outside with her friends at 3:00. At 3:30 they came back inside. For how many minutes did they skate?
   30

3. Mark and his mother went outside to look at the stars through their telescope. It started getting dark at 7:00. By 8:00 they went inside. How long were they looking at stars? one hour

4. Tasha's new kitten loves to play with a ball of yarn. But by 4:30 she was fast asleep in Tasha's lap. The kitten played with the yarn for a quarter-hour. What time did she start? 4:15

5. Eva and her father worked on a model rocket together. The fins were hard to attach. By 11:30, they had worked on the fins for a half-hour. What time did they begin? 11:00

Page 11

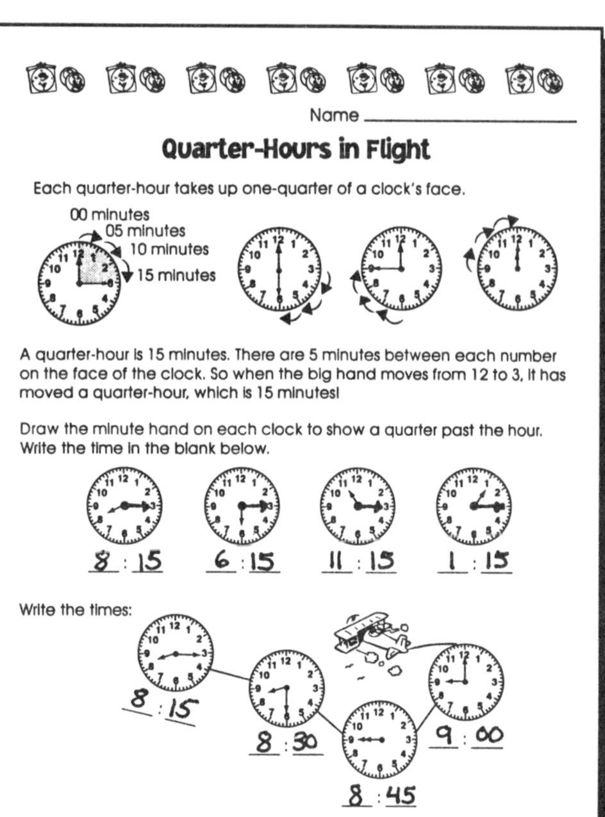

Name ______________

Quarter-Hours in Flight

Each quarter-hour takes up one-quarter of a clock's face.

A quarter-hour is 15 minutes. There are 5 minutes between each number on the face of the clock. So when the big hand moves from 12 to 3, it has moved a quarter-hour, which is 15 minutes!

Draw the minute hand on each clock to show a quarter past the hour. Write the time in the blank below.

8 : 15 6 : 15 11 : 15 1 : 15

Write the times:

8 : 15 8 : 30 8 : 45 9 : 00

Page 12

Quarter Hours in Flight cont. Name ______________

Time is really "flying by" here! Identify each quarter-hour as it flies by. Write the correct time in each blank.

2 : 00 2 : 15 2 : 30

9 : 15 9 : 30

7 : 15 7 : 45 7 : 30

Page 13

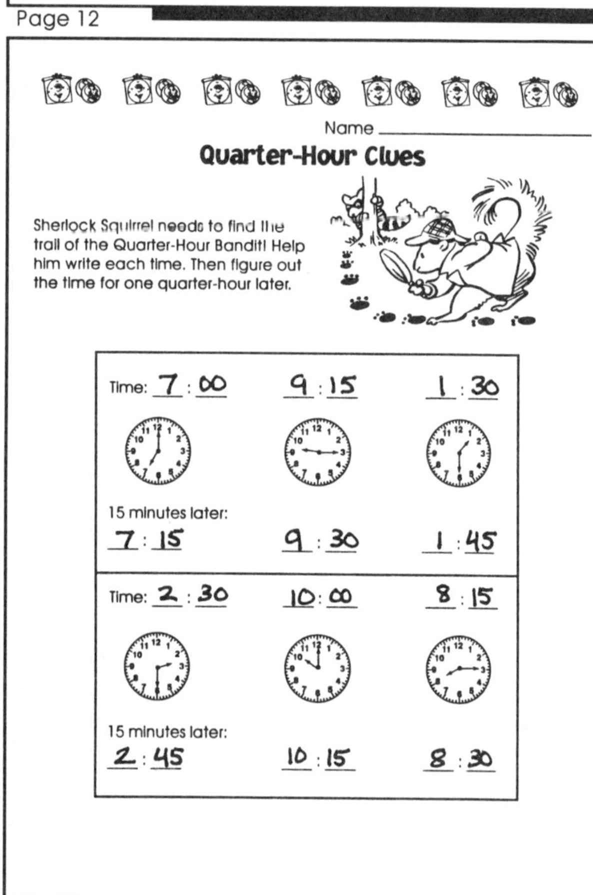

Name ______________

Quarter-Hour Clues

Sherlock Squirrel needs to find the trail of the Quarter-Hour Bandit! Help him write each time. Then figure out the time for one quarter-hour later.

Time: 7 : 00	9 : 15	1 : 30
15 minutes later: 7 : 15	9 : 30	1 : 45
Time: 2 : 30	10 : 00	8 : 15
15 minutes later: 2 : 45	10 : 15	8 : 30

Page 14

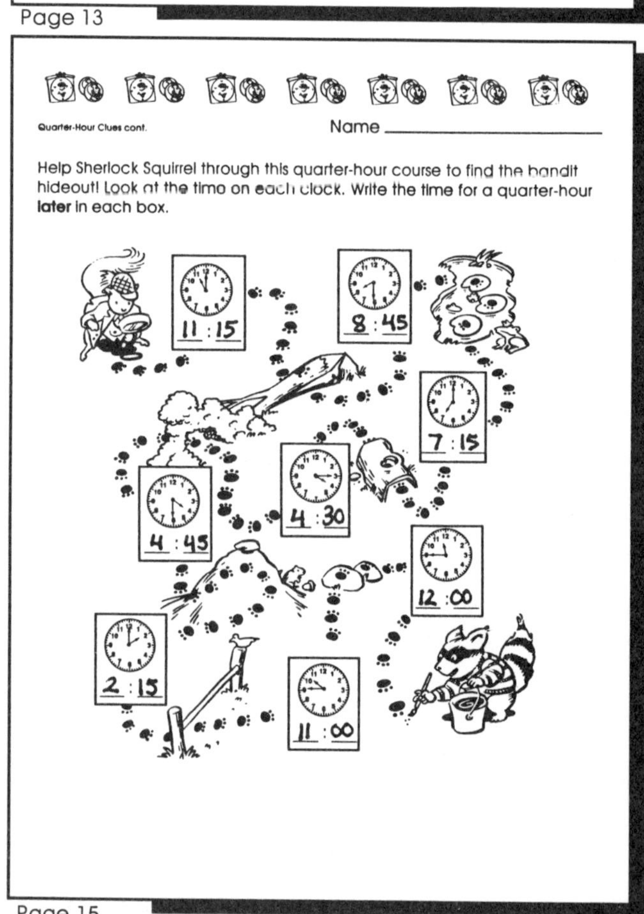

Quarter-Hour Clues cont. Name ______________

Help Sherlock Squirrel through this quarter-hour course to find the bandit hideout! Look at the time on each clock. Write the time for a quarter-hour **later** in each box.

11 : 15 8 : 45 7 : 15 4 : 30 4 : 45 12 : 00 2 : 15 11 : 00

Page 15

Name ______________

Quarter-Hour Art Class

Read the story problems. Then write the correct times in the blanks.

1. In art class, Mark started drawing a ranch at 1:00. It took him a quarter-hour to draw a horse. What time did he finish his horse? 1 : 15
2. The teacher told Chung to wait a quarter-hour to let the glue dry on her collage. She started working again at 1:30. What time did she stop to let the glue dry? 1 : 15

3. David spilled some paint, and it took him a quarter-hour to clean it up. He started cleaning at 1:30. What time did he finish? 1 : 45
4. Martha was asked to help pick up art supplies. She got everything put away by 2:00. It took her a quarter-hour. What time did she start? 1 : 45

Page 16

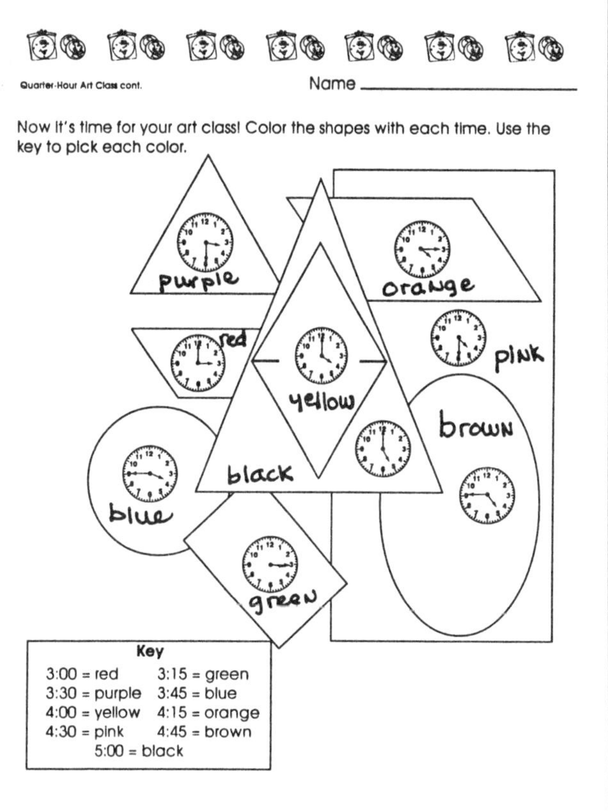

Quarter-Hour Art Class cont.
Name
Now it's time for your art class! Color the shapes with each time. Use the key to pick each color.
purple
orange
red
yellow
pink
brown
blue
black
green
Key
3:00 = red
3:15 = green
3:30 = purple
3:45 = blue
4:00 = yellow
4:15 = orange
4:30 = pink
4:45 = brown
5:00 = black

Page 17

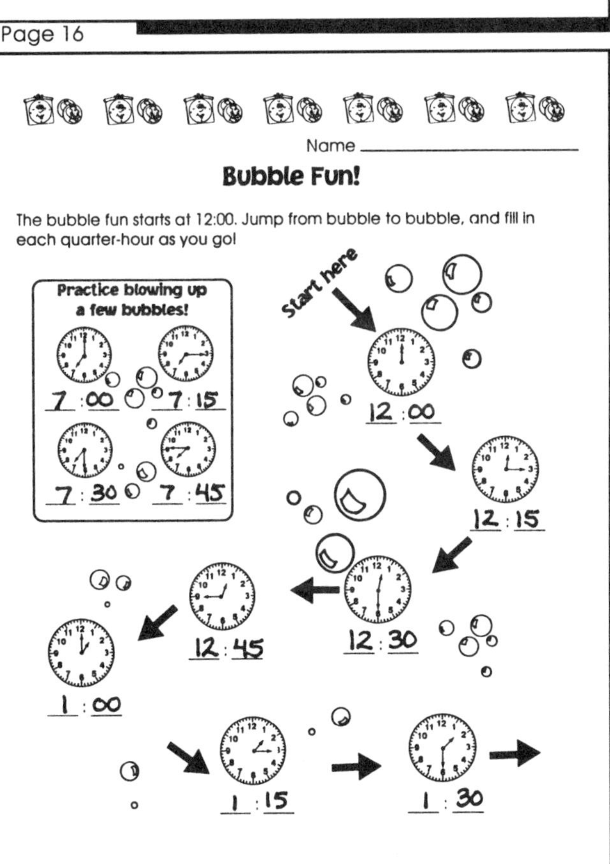

Name
Bubble Fun!
The bubble fun starts at 12:00. Jump from bubble to bubble, and fill in each quarter-hour as you go!
Practice blowing up a few bubbles!
7:00
7:15
7:30
7:45
Start here
12:00
12:15
12:30
12:45
1:00
1:15
1:30

Page 18

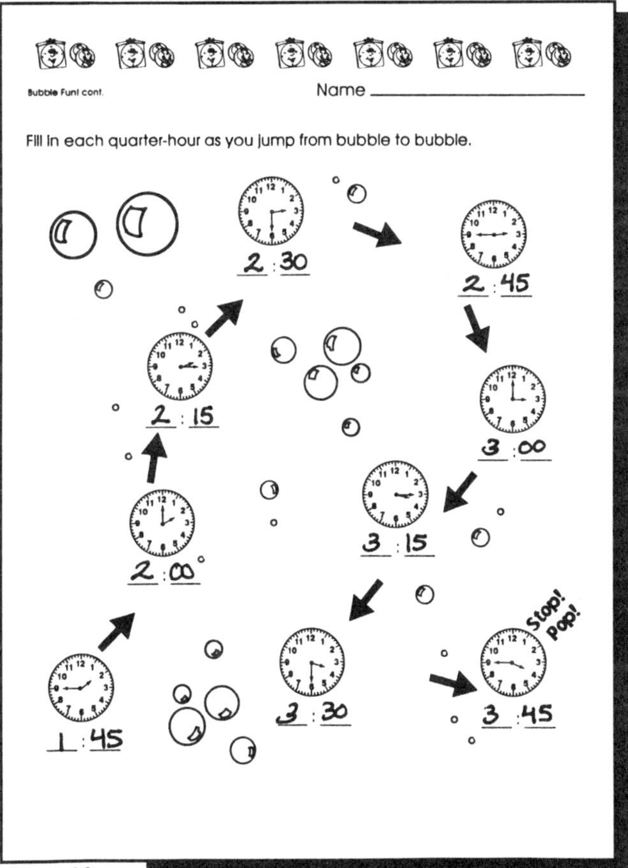

Page 19

Name ____________

Five Is the Key

It takes five minutes for the minute hand to move from one number to another. Start at the 12 and count by 5s.

You can read minutes easily by counting by 5s. For example, when the minute hand is on the 4, it's 20 minutes past the hour.

Count by 5s. Write the minutes under each clock.

3 : 25

10 : 40

12 : 10

8 : 55

12 : 45

9 : 50

Page 20

Name ____________

Adding Up the Minutes

Help Chung keep track of time. Write the correct time beneath each clock.

1. Chung leaves her house at 9:00. It takes her 10 minutes to walk to Maria's house. What time does she arrive?

9 : 10

2. Maria shows Chung the new kittens. They play with the kittens for 25 minutes. What time do they stop?

9 : 35

3. Then Maria and Chung go outside to play in Maria's swimming pool. They swim for 45 minutes. What time do they get out of the pool?

10 : 20

4. Chung and Maria walk to their school to play on the playground. They leave at 10:45. It takes them 5 minutes to walk to the school. What time do they arrive?

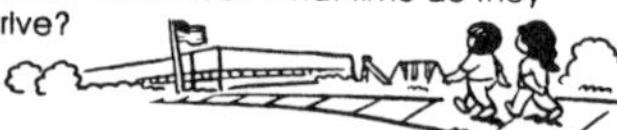

10 : 50

Page 21

Name ____________

Time Travel

Every day, we travel through time! Follow Alesha through her day. Write each time.

Alesha gets on her bike at 9 : 00.

Five minutes later, she is at her grandfather's house. 9 : 05

Today is a special day. It's Grandpa's birthday! He opens his card at 9 : 15.

Grandpa takes Alesha out to breakfast at 9 : 30.

Since it's his birthday, Grandpa orders pancakes!

Page 22

Name ____________

Time Travel Too

Write the times as David writes his story!

David sits down to write a new story at 4 : 00.

He is writing a story about puppies. David writes for 15 minutes. 4 : 15

David feels a tug on his jeans. He pretends not to notice for 5 minutes, until 4 : 20.

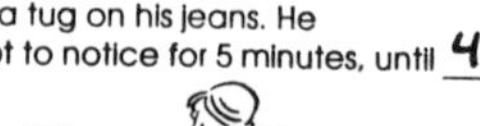

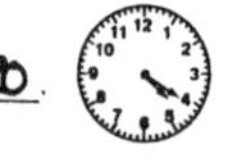

It's his new puppy, Chiggles! David decides to play with her for a half-hour, until 4 : 50.

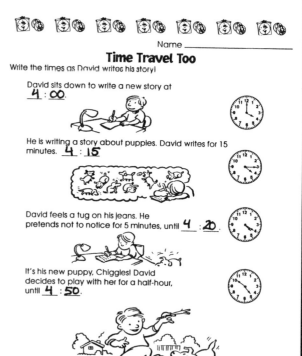

Page 23

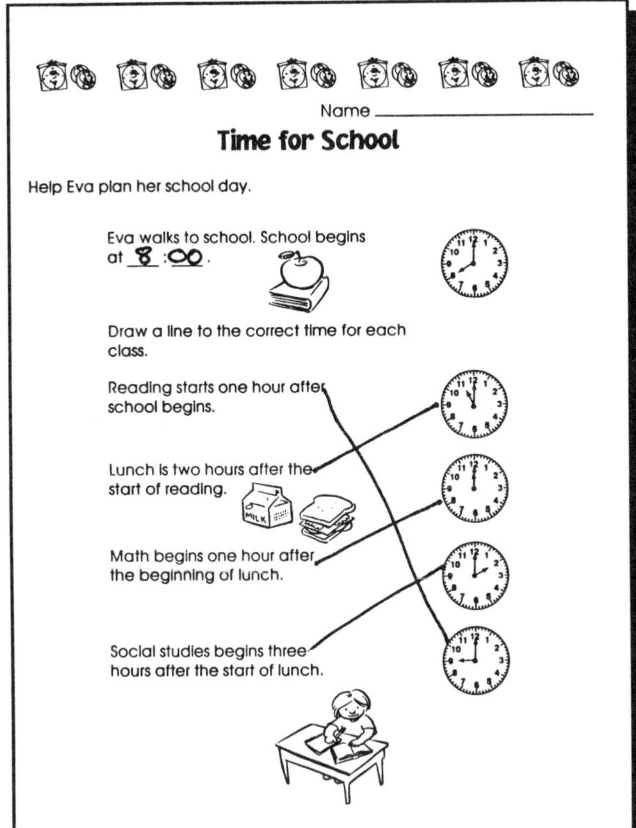

Name __________________

Time for School

Help Eva plan her school day.

Eva walks to school. School begins at 8 : 00.

Draw a line to the correct time for each class.

Reading starts one hour after school begins.

Lunch is two hours after the start of reading.

Math begins one hour after the beginning of lunch.

Social studies begins three hours after the start of lunch.

Page 24

Name __________________

Fun Day

Each person here spent one hour at a Fun Day activity. They started at different times. Write the times when they were done in the spaces.

Sam went on the bumper car ride from 1:00 to 2 : 00.

Pedro started playing hockey at 1:30. He was done at 2 : 30.

Chung made chalk drawings from 2:30 to 3 : 30.

Eva rode a unicycle! She rode from 3:00 to 4 : 00.

David played marbles from 2:15 to 3 : 15.

Page 25

Name __________________

School Picnic Time

Join the school picnic! You can be the timekeeper.

Calculate how much time each activity took. Write your answers in the blanks.

1. David and Anna May played volleyball from 1:20 till 1:40. They played 20 minutes.
2. Alesha rode a pony for 25 minutes. She began at 1:00. She finished at 1 : 25.
3. Alesha had so much fun that she stayed for another 15 minutes! She finished her second pony ride at 1 : 40.

Page 26

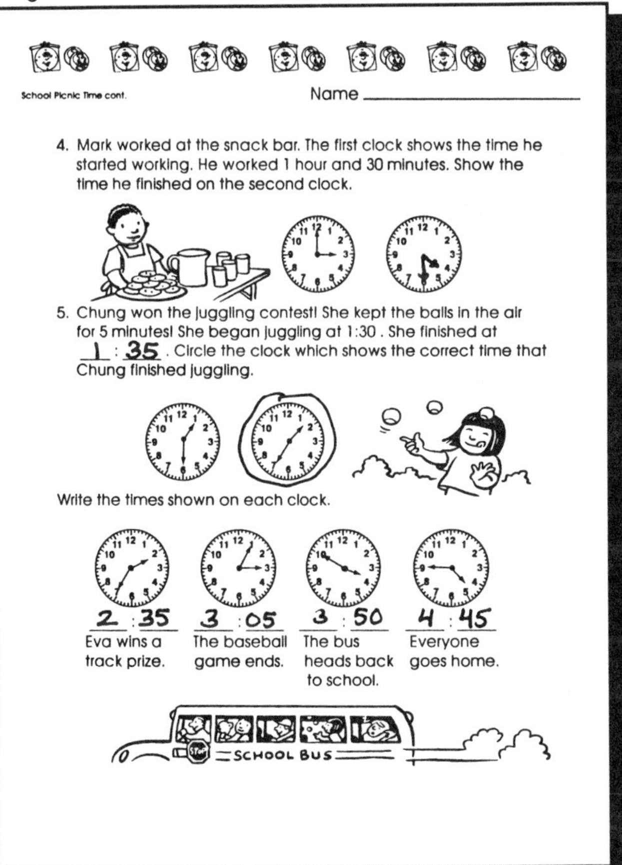

School Picnic Time cont.

Name __________________

4. Mark worked at the snack bar. The first clock shows the time he started working. He worked 1 hour and 30 minutes. Show the time he finished on the second clock.
5. Chung won the juggling contest! She kept the balls in the air for 5 minutes! She began juggling at 1:30 . She finished at 1 : 35 . Circle the clock which shows the correct time that Chung finished juggling.

Write the times shown on each clock.

2 : 35	3 : 05	3 : 50	4 : 45
Eva wins a track prize.	The baseball game ends.	The bus heads back to school.	Everyone goes home.

Page 27

Name ______________________

Break the Codes!

Can you read these secret messages? You can if you can read the time!

Write the correct time under each clock. Then match the letter of that clock to a space below. When all the blanks are filled in, read the message!

Question: Who will tell if you are late?

L = 8:15

E = 7:25

T = 6:05

! = 11:55

M = 3:25

W = 4:10

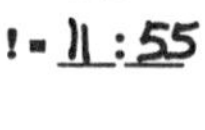

I = 8:40

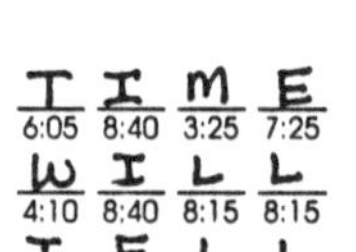

T I M E
6:05 8:40 3:25 7:25

W I L L
4:10 8:40 8:15 8:15

T E L L !
6:05 7:25 8:15 8:15 11:55

Page 28

Break the Codes cont.

Name ______________________

Write the correct time under each clock. Then match the letter of each clock to a space below.

Question: How do we know that time is as light as air?

E = 1:00

L = 7:55

T = 6:40

M = 3:45

I = 7:25

F = 10:30

E = 4:55

S = 9:15

I = 12:00

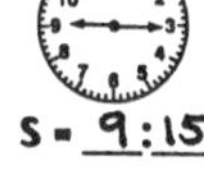

Because

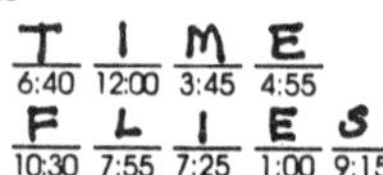

T I M E
6:40 12:00 3:45 4:55

F L I E S.
10:30 7:55 7:25 1:00 9:15

Page 29

Name ______________________

Time Never Stops

Let's say that it is 1:00. Thirty minutes from now it will be 1:30. Thirty minutes from 1:30, it will be 2:00. Time keeps moving. Write the time shown on the clock face. Then write the time a half-hour earlier or later, as shown.

10 : 00 + 30 minutes
= 10 : 30

3 : 00 + 30 minutes
= 3 : 30

1 : 15 - 30 minutes
= 12 : 45

6 : 00 + 30 minutes
= 6 : 30

7 : 30 + 30 minutes
= 8 : 00

9 : 15 - 30 minutes
= 8 : 45

How many minutes are there in each half-hour?

15 (30) 60

Page 30

Name ______________________

Game Time

This is "Tick, Tack, Clock"! To win this game, find three clocks that are showing quarter-hours! Write each time. Find the three quarter-hour clocks and draw a line right through them!

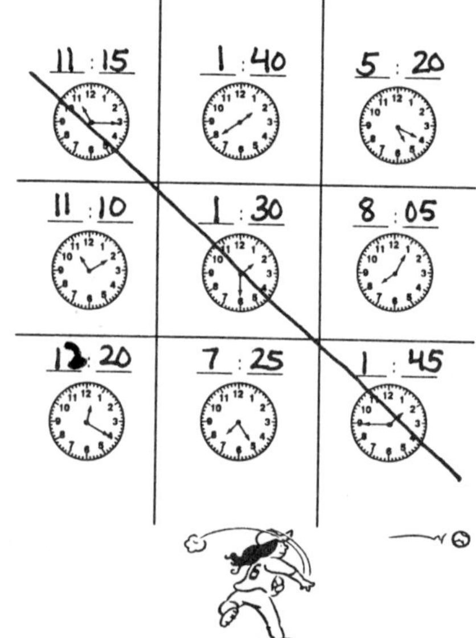

31

Name ______________________

Welcome to Class!

Here are all the things that happened in a classroom today. Keep track of time as it passes by writing down the correct time after each event.

1. Class started when Mrs. Andrews introduced the new class pet! **8:00**
   The students spent 10 minutes meeting Jerry the Gerbil. What time were they done? 8 : 10

2. Martha shared a book with the class about colorful animals that live around the world. **9:00**

   It took Martha 20 minutes to show her book to everyone. When did they finish? 9 : 20

3. Monica shared birthday treats with her class. Everyone loved them! **10:15**

   The class finished the treats in 10 minutes. What time were they done?
   10 : 25

4. Eva gave her report on frogs during science. **11:00**

   Eva took 15 minutes to give her report. When did she finish? 11 : 15

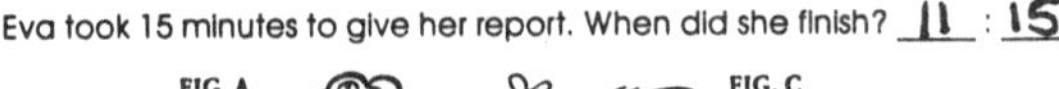

Page 32

Welcome to Class! cont.

Name ______________________

5. David worked on a fort outside during recess. **1:30**
   Recess was 20 minutes. What time did David stop?
   1 : 50

6. Pedro painted a picture of his house during art class. He used colored sand to cover the outside. **2:00**

   Pedro worked on his picture for 40 minutes. What time was he done?
   2 : 40

7. Chung made a reed flute during art class. She wrapped it in paper to take it home. **2:55**

   Chung was ready to catch the bus in 5 minutes. What time did she finish wrapping her flute? 3 : 00

8. If Chung's bus ride home took 15 minutes, what time did she get home?
   3 : 15

Page 33

Name ______________________

Chart It!

On the planet Zotz, Mrs. Bleepz has made a chart to help her remember her children's schedules. Read the chart. Then answer the questions on page 35.

	Blurp	Zeezo	Bleeza
Ride transport to school	7:30	8:00	8:15
Home from school	3:15	4:00	3:45
Zeek-X practice	4:30	—	4:45
Flugle lesson	—	4:30	5:30
Starts homework	5:30	7:30	7:00

Page 34

Chart It! cont.

Name ______________________

Write the time.

1. When does Blurp ride the transport? 7 : 30
2. When does Bleeza get home from school? 3 : 45
3. What time does Zeezo go to his flugle lesson? 4 : 00
4. If Bleeza has an hour of homework, what time will she be done? 7 : 30
5. What time does Zeezo start his homework? 7 : 30

Circle the right answer.

6. Who goes to a flugle lesson first?
   Blurp (Zeezo) Bleeza
7. Who gets home first?
   (Blurp) Zeezo Bleeza
8. Who plays Zeek-X at 4:30?
   (Blurp) Zeezo Bleeza
9. Who rides the transport first?
   (Blurp) Zeezo Bleeza

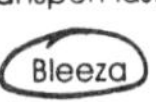

10. Who rides the transport last?
    Blurp Zeezo (Bleeza)

Do you see why Mrs. Bleepz needs a chart?

Page 35

Name ______________

Just a Minute!

How long is a minute? It zooms by! Circle each activity that only takes one minute.

Name ______________

A Minute at a Time

If the minute hand points to the first mark right after the **12**, that means it is 1 minute past the hour.

If the minute had points to the mark right after the **1**, that means it is 5 minutes + 1 minute past the hour, or __6__ minutes.

If the minute hand points to the mark right after the **2**, that means it is __11__ minutes past the hour.

Try these:

__16__ minutes after the hour.

__9__ minutes after the hour.

__11__ minutes after the hour.

Name ______________

Digital Minutes!

It is easier to tell time to the minute on a digital clock face. If the digital clock read 12:06, that means it is 6 minutes past 12. A digital clock counts minutes for you.

Draw a line from each clock on the left to a clock on the right that is one minute later.

Left	Right
12:00	5:01
5:00	10:01
7:00	12:01
8:00	8:01
10:00	7:01
11:00	3:01
3:00	11:01

Name ______________

One Minute Later

Write the correct times.

1. It takes Mark one minute to run from the basement to the attic. If he starts at 1:06, what time will he get to the attic? __1__ : __07__

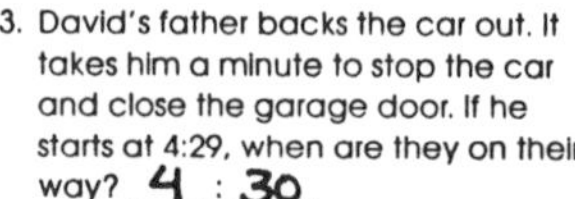

2. At 6:02, Maria's mother calls out, "The pizza is here!" Her brothers are there a minute later, at __6__ : __03__.

3. David's father backs the car out. It takes him a minute to stop the car and close the garage door. If he starts at 4:29, when are they on their way? __4__ : __30__

4. Chung can draw a picture of a rabbit in one minute. She starts at 10:09. What time is she done? __10__ : __10__

5. The bus picks up Eva at 7:47. If she is a minute early, what time does she get to her bus stop? __7__ : __46__

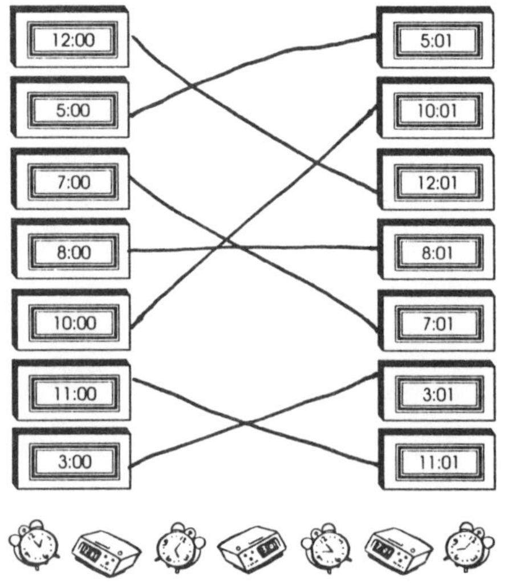

Name ____________________

Early, Late, or On Time?

Imagine you are going to a birthday party. It starts at 2:00.

If you arrive at the party at 2:00, we say you are "on time."

If you arrive **before** 2:00, you are **early**.

If you arrive after 2:00, you are **late**.

Circle the correct time.

Kim eats dinner at 5:30. Circle the clock that shows a time when dinner at her house was **early**.

 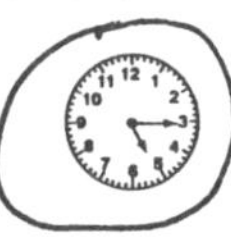 

Circle the correct answer: If Kim's dinner is served on time, and she got home from Girl Scouts at 5:40, would she be

early 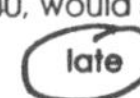 **late** **on time**

Page 40

Name ____________________

Are They on Time?

Circle the correct times.

1. Chung goes to her piano lesson at 4:00. Circle the clock that shows she was **on time**.

2. David's school starts at 8:00. Circle the clock that shows he was **late**.

3. Maria feeds her kitten at 7:00. Circle the clock that shows she was **early**.

 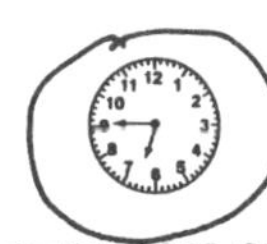 

4. Earl had to go to the dentist at 3:15. Circle the clock that shows he was **on time**.

Page 41

Name ____________________

7 Days = 1 Week

Let's see how much you know about the days of the week!

Sunday	Monday	Tuesday	Wednesday	Thursday	Friday	Saturday
1	2	3	4	5	6	7

1. Circle the first day of the week:

 Sunday Monday Thursday Wednesday

2. Circle the last day of the week:

Friday Saturday

3. Which day has the most letters in its name?
Wednesday

4. The hour hand goes all the way around the clock twice during one day. How many hours are there in one day? 24

5. Which two days make up the weekend?
Saturday Sunday

6. What is the third day of the week?
Tuesday

7. Write the name of your favorite day of the week:
Answers will vary.

Page 42

Name ____________________

All in One Week

Fill in each blank below. Use the clue to find each day of the week.

1. Earl plays soccer on Friday (sixth day).

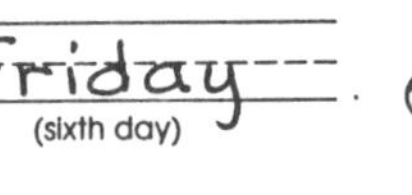

2. Monica has dance class every Tuesday (third day).

3. Pedro rides his bike to the park on Saturday (seventh day).

4. Maria has swimming lessons on Thursday (fifth day).

5. Tammy never misses choir practice on Wednesday (fourth day).

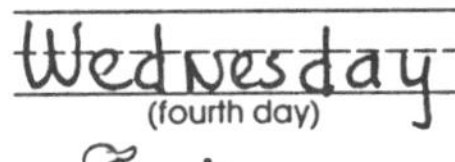

6. Jacob's first day of school was Monday (second day).

Page 43

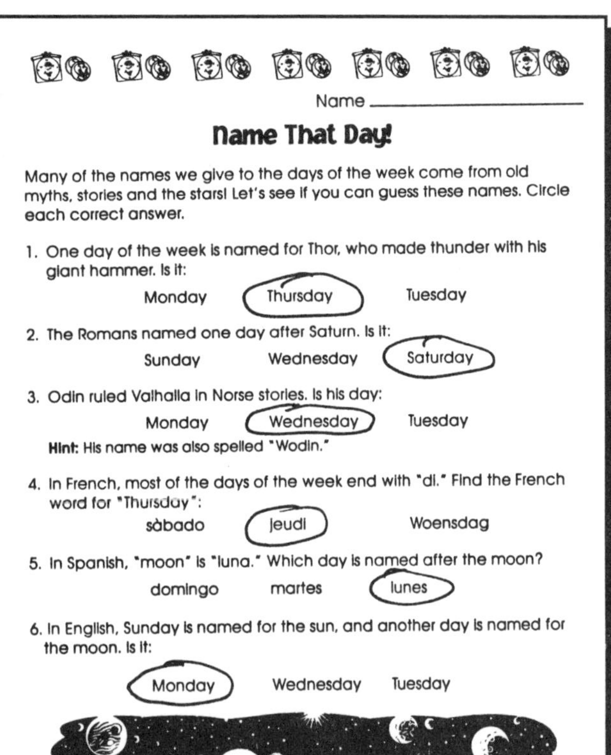

Name ____________

Name That Day!

Many of the names we give to the days of the week come from old myths, stories and the stars! Let's see if you can guess these names. Circle each correct answer.

1. One day of the week is named for Thor, who made thunder with his giant hammer. Is it:
   Monday **(Thursday)** Tuesday
2. The Romans named one day after Saturn. Is it:
   Sunday Wednesday **(Saturday)**
3. Odin ruled Valhalla in Norse stories. Is his day:
   Monday **(Wednesday)** Tuesday
   Hint: His name was also spelled "Wodin."
4. In French, most of the days of the week end with "di." Find the French word for "Thursday":
   sàbado **(jeudi)** Woensdag
5. In Spanish, "moon" is "luna." Which day is named after the moon?
   domingo martes **(lunes)**
6. In English, Sunday is named for the sun, and another day is named for the moon. Is it:
   (Monday) Wednesday Tuesday

Page 44

Name ____________

Isabel's First Week

Write the correct days of the week in each blank to complete the story. Use the clues to help you.

The new baby was born on (third day) Tuesday. The next day, (fourth day) Wednesday, we decided to name her Isabel.

Mom and Isabel came home from the hospital on (fifth day) Thursday. Two days later, (seventh day), Saturday everybody came over to meet her!

Aunt Silvia and Uncle Frank had flown from Portland the day before, on (sixth day) Friday. Grandma and Grandpa came over. So did Uncle Joe, and my cousins Rose and Robert.

I guess Isabel got tired out from all the people. On the day after the party, (first day) Sunday, she cried almost all morning!

She was better a day later, on (second day) Monday. That's when I brought Chung over to see my new sister. We made silly faces. Isabel smiled!

Page 45

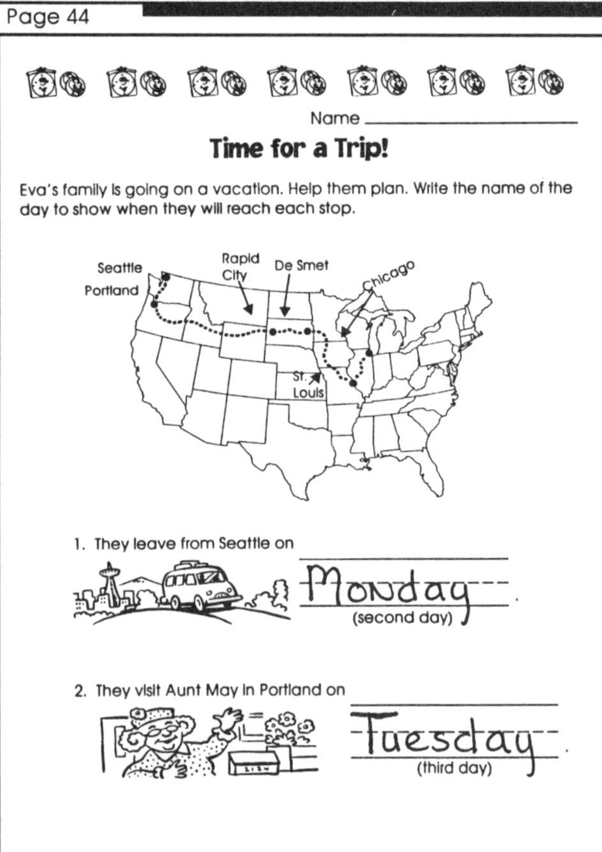

Name ____________

Time for a Trip!

Eva's family is going on a vacation. Help them plan. Write the name of the day to show when they will reach each stop.

Seattle
Portland
Rapid City
De Smet
Chicago
St. Louis

1. They leave from Seattle on Monday (second day).
2. They visit Aunt May in Portland on Tuesday (third day).

Page 46

Time for a Trip! cont. Name ____________

Sunday	Monday	Tuesday	Wednesday	Thursday	Friday	Saturday
1	2	3	4	5	6	7

3. They go to Mount Rushmore near Rapid City on

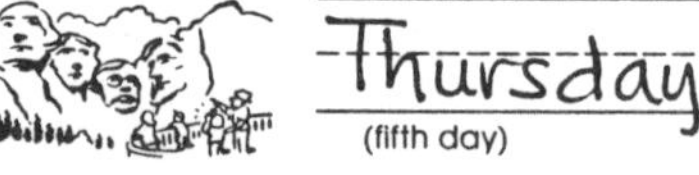

Thursday (fifth day).

4. They see Laura Ingalls Wilder's home in De Smet on

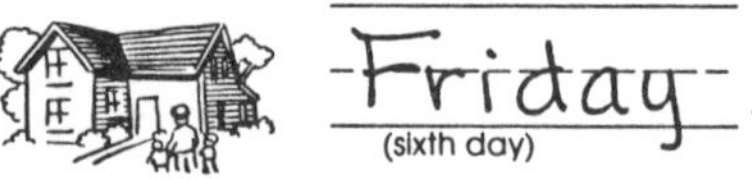

Friday (sixth day).

5. They take a riverboat tour in St. Louis on

Saturday (seventh day).

6. They go to a baseball game in Chicago on

Sunday (first day).

Eva thinks it's the best vacation her family has ever had!

Page 47

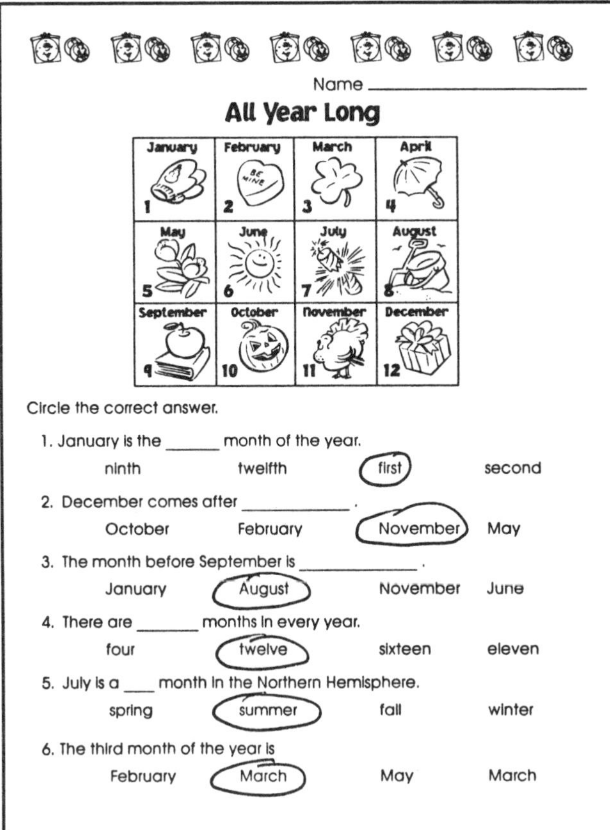

Name ____________________

All Year Long

January	February	March	April
1	2	3	4
May	**June**	**July**	**August**
5	6	7	8
September	**October**	**November**	**December**
9	10	11	12

Circle the correct answer.

1. January is the ______ month of the year.
   ninth twelfth **first** (circled) second
2. December comes after ____________.
   October February **November** (circled) May
3. The month before September is ____________.
   January **August** (circled) November June
4. There are _______ months in every year.
   four **twelve** (circled) sixteen eleven
5. July is a ___ month in the Northern Hemisphere.
   spring **summer** (circled) fall winter
6. The third month of the year is
   February **March** (circled) May March

Page 48

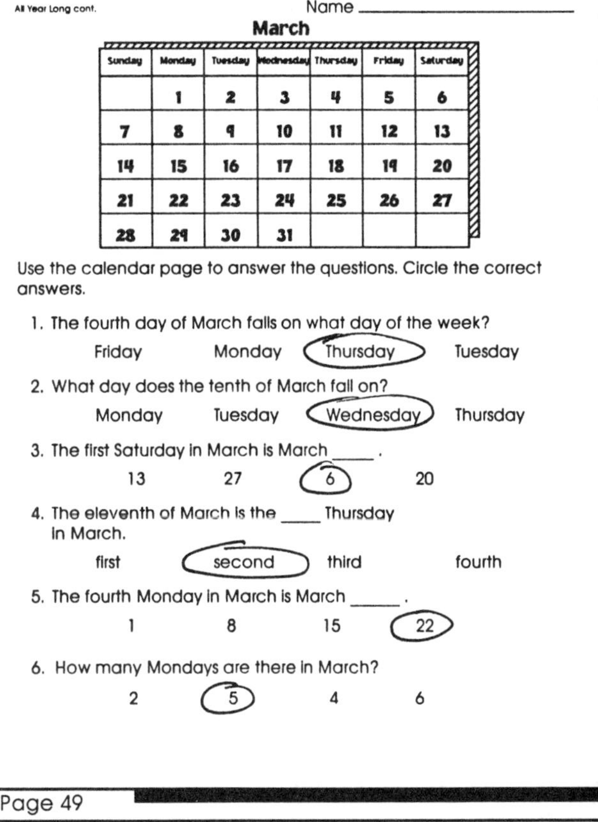

Name ____________________

All Year Long cont.

March

Sunday	Monday	Tuesday	Wednesday	Thursday	Friday	Saturday
	1	2	3	4	5	6
7	8	9	10	11	12	13
14	15	16	17	18	19	20
21	22	23	24	25	26	27
28	29	30	31			

Use the calendar page to answer the questions. Circle the correct answers.

1. The fourth day of March falls on what day of the week?
   Friday Monday **Thursday** (circled) Tuesday
2. What day does the tenth of March fall on?
   Monday Tuesday **Wednesday** (circled) Thursday
3. The first Saturday in March is March _____.
   13 27 **6** (circled) 20
4. The eleventh of March is the _____ Thursday in March.
   first **second** (circled) third fourth
5. The fourth Monday in March is March _____.
   1 8 15 **22** (circled)
6. How many Mondays are there in March?
   2 **5** (circled) 4 6

Page 49

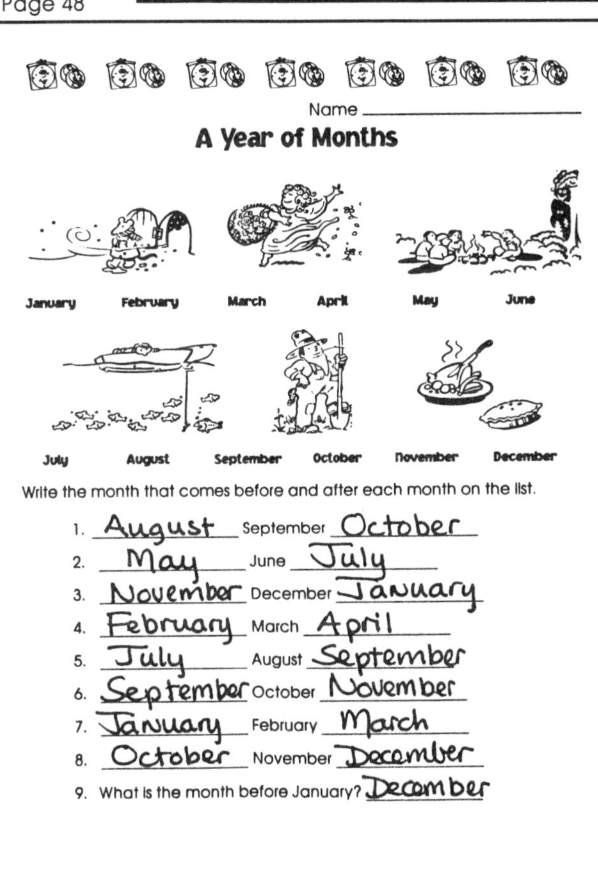

Name ____________________

A Year of Months

Write the month that comes before and after each month on the list.

1. August September October
2. May June July
3. November December January
4. February March April
5. July August September
6. September October November
7. January February March
8. October November December
9. What is the month before January? December

Page 50

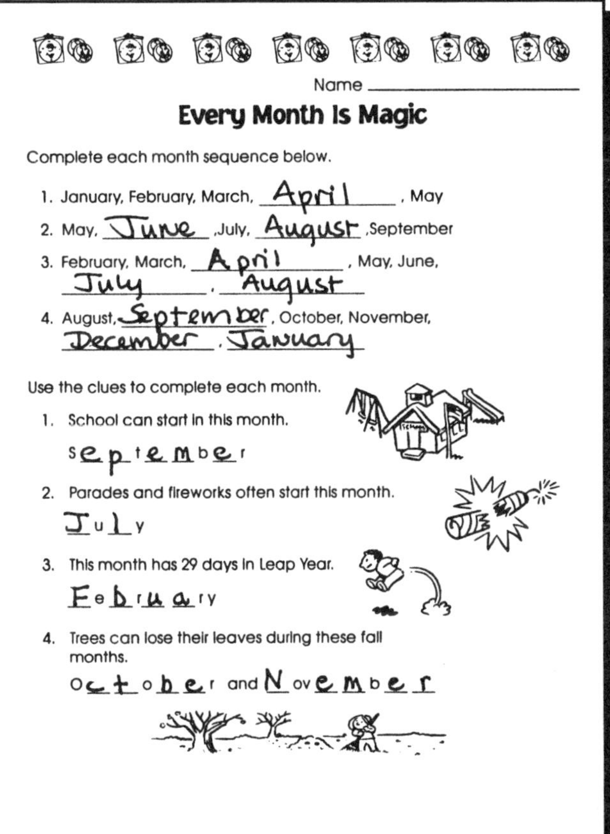

Name ____________________

Every Month Is Magic

Complete each month sequence below.

1. January, February, March, April, May
2. May, June, July, August, September
3. February, March, April, May, June, July, August
4. August, September, October, November, December, January

Use the clues to complete each month.

1. School can start in this month.
   September
2. Parades and fireworks often start this month.
   July
3. This month has 29 days in Leap Year.
   February
4. Trees can lose their leaves during these fall months.
   October and November

Page 51

Name ____________

Let's Plan a Month

Sunday	Monday	Tuesday	Wednesday	Thursday	Friday	Saturday
					1	2 Concert
3 Family party for Chung	4	5 Chung's birthday	6	7	8	9 Maria's sledding party
10	11 Teacher conference	12	13	14	15	16
17 Go to Grandma's for dinner	18	19	20 Science Fair	21	22	23
24/31	25	26 Field trip	27	28 Winter break	29 Winter break	30

Here is Mrs. Lee's calendar for January. Use it to answer the questions. Circle the correct answers.

1. What day of the week is Chung's birthday?
   Sunday Tuesday Wednesday Saturday
2. What is the date of the concert?
   January 2 January 4 January 5 January 6
3. What day of the week is Maria's sledding party?
   Friday Saturday Sunday Monday
4. What is the date of Chung's field trip?
   January 21 January 26 January 30 January 25
5. What is the day of Chung's field trip?
   Monday Tuesday Wednesday Thursday

Page 52

Let's Plan a Month cont

Name ____________

Write the answers to the questions. Use the calendar on page 52.

6. Write the date of the Science Fair. January 20
7. What day of the week does Mrs. Lee have a teacher conference? Monday
8. What day of the week is the Lee family going to Grandma's for dinner? Sunday
9. What is the date of Chung's birthday? January 5
10. What day of the week is Chung's family giving her a party? Sunday
11. What are the two days of the week when Chung has winter break? Thursday and Friday
12. What is the date of Chung's last day of school before winter break? January 27
13. On what day of the week does February start? Monday

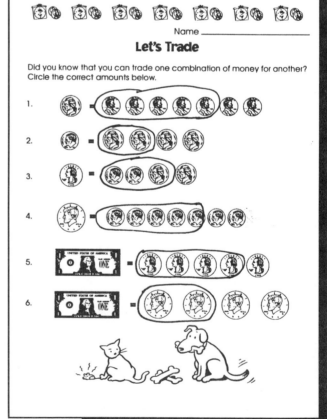

Page 53

Name ____________

It's Your Money!

Circle the correct answers.

1. Here's a penny. It is worth ______ cent.
   1 5 10 25 50
2. Remember the nickel? It's worth ______ cents.
   1 5 10 25 50
3. The smallest coin is the dime. It is worth ______ cents.
   1 5 10 25 50
4. The quarter is ¼ of a dollar, or ______ cents.
   1 5 10 25 50
5. The rare half-dollar is worth ______ cents.
   1 5 10 25 50
6. The dollar is paper. It is worth ______ cents.
   50 100 500 1,000

Page 54

Name ____________

Let's Trade

Did you know that you can trade one combination of money for another? Circle the correct amounts below.

1.

2.

3.

4.

5.

6.

Page 55

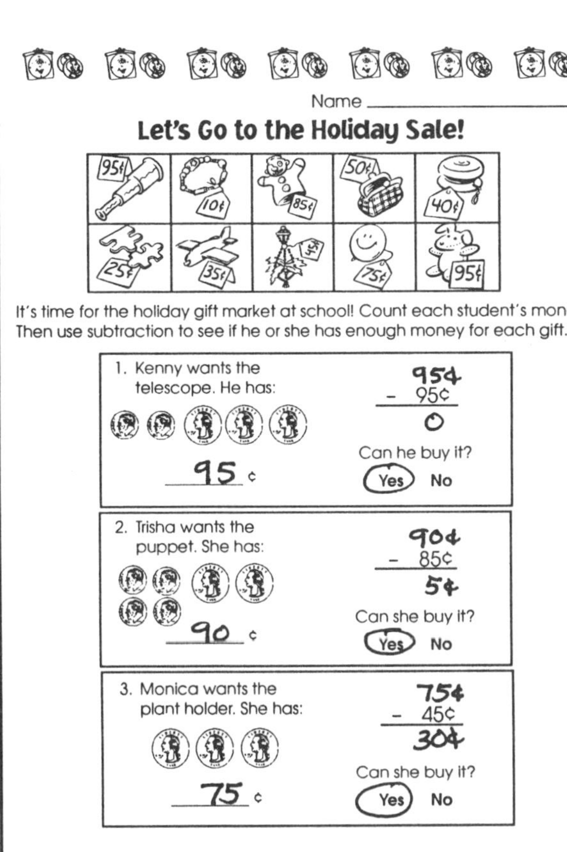

Name ______________

Let's Go to the Holiday Sale!

95¢ 10¢ 85¢ 50¢ 40¢
25¢ 35¢ 45¢ 75¢ 95¢

It's time for the holiday gift market at school! Count each student's money. Then use subtraction to see if he or she has enough money for each gift.

1. Kenny wants the telescope. He has: 95 ¢ — 95¢ − 95¢ = 0. Can he buy it? **Yes** No
2. Trisha wants the puppet. She has: 90 ¢ — 90¢ − 85¢ = 5¢. Can she buy it? **Yes** No
3. Monica wants the plant holder. She has: 75 ¢ — 75¢ − 45¢ = 30¢. Can she buy it? **Yes** No

Page 56

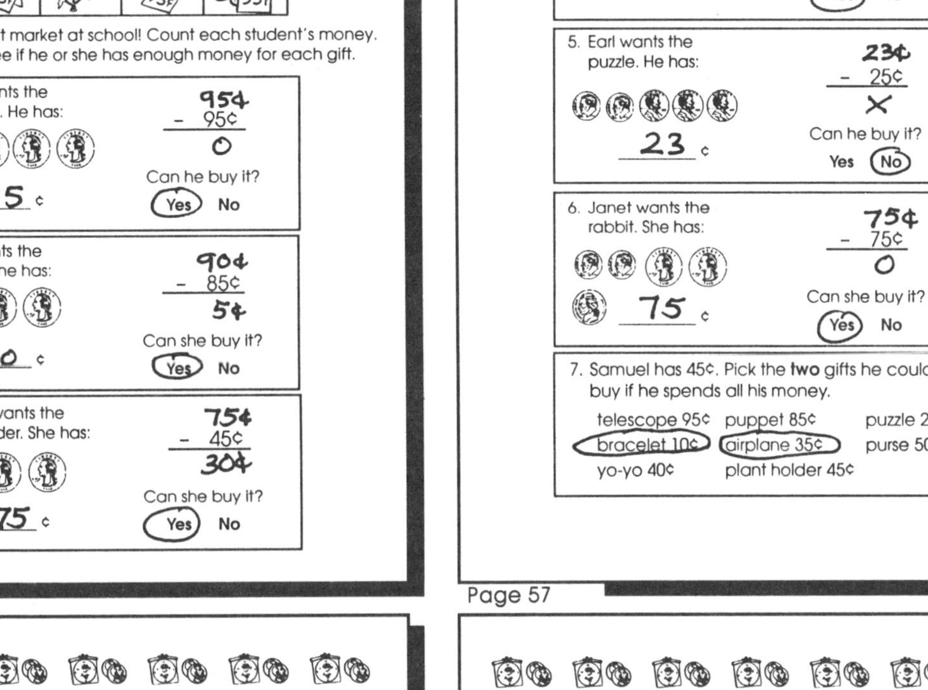

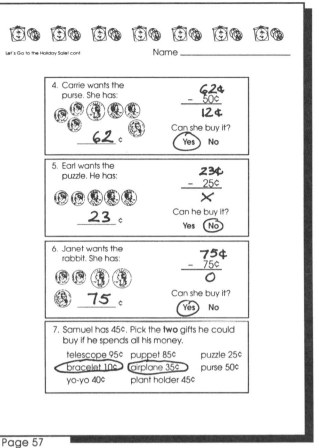

Let's Go to the Holiday Sale! cont

Name ______________

4. Carrie wants the purse. She has: 62 ¢ — 62¢ − 50¢ = 12¢. Can she buy it? **Yes** No
5. Earl wants the puzzle. He has: 23 ¢ — 23¢ − 25¢ = X. Can he buy it? Yes **No**
6. Janet wants the rabbit. She has: 75 ¢ — 75¢ − 75¢ = 0. Can she buy it? **Yes** No
7. Samuel has 45¢. Pick the **two** gifts he could buy if he spends all his money.

telescope 95¢ puppet 85¢ puzzle 25¢
bracelet 10¢ **airplane 35¢** purse 50¢
yo-yo 40¢ plant holder 45¢

Page 57

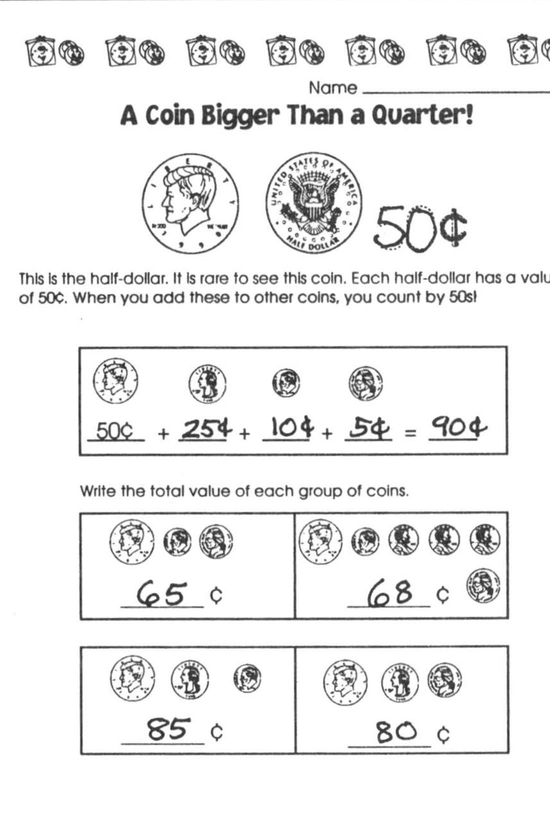

Name ______________

A Coin Bigger Than a Quarter!

50¢

This is the half-dollar. It is rare to see this coin. Each half-dollar has a value of 50¢. When you add these to other coins, you count by 50s!

50¢ + 25¢ + 10¢ + 5¢ = 90¢

Write the total value of each group of coins.

65 ¢ 68 ¢
85 ¢ 80 ¢

Page 58

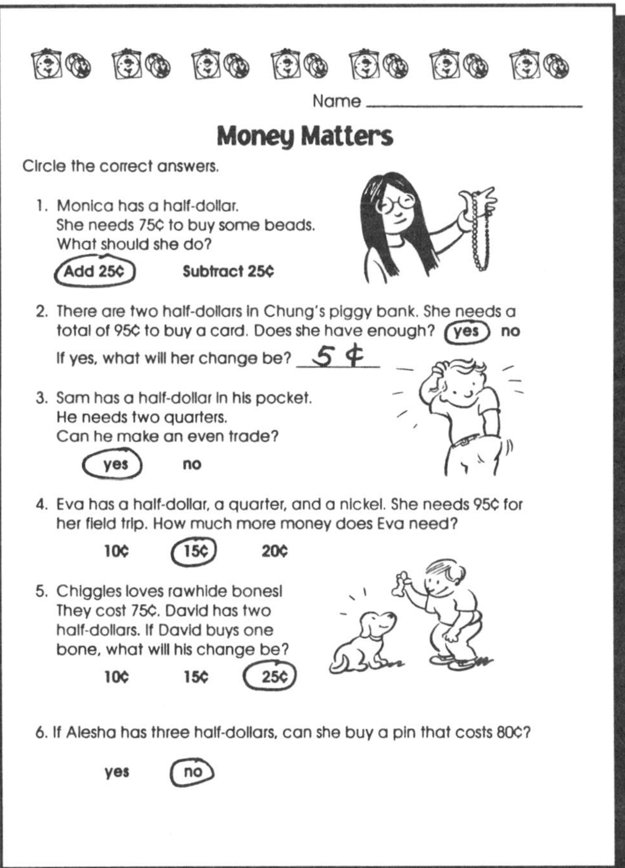

Name ______________

Money Matters

Circle the correct answers.

1. Monica has a half-dollar. She needs 75¢ to buy some beads. What should she do?
   Add 25¢ Subtract 25¢
2. There are two half-dollars in Chung's piggy bank. She needs a total of 95¢ to buy a card. Does she have enough? **yes** no
   If yes, what will her change be? 5 ¢
3. Sam has a half-dollar in his pocket. He needs two quarters. Can he make an even trade?
   yes no
4. Eva has a half-dollar, a quarter, and a nickel. She needs 95¢ for her field trip. How much more money does Eva need?
   10¢ **15¢** 20¢
5. Chiggles loves rawhide bones! They cost 75¢. David has two half-dollars. If David buys one bone, what will his change be?
   10¢ 15¢ **25¢**
6. If Alesha has three half-dollars, can she buy a pin that costs 80¢?
   yes **no**

Page 59

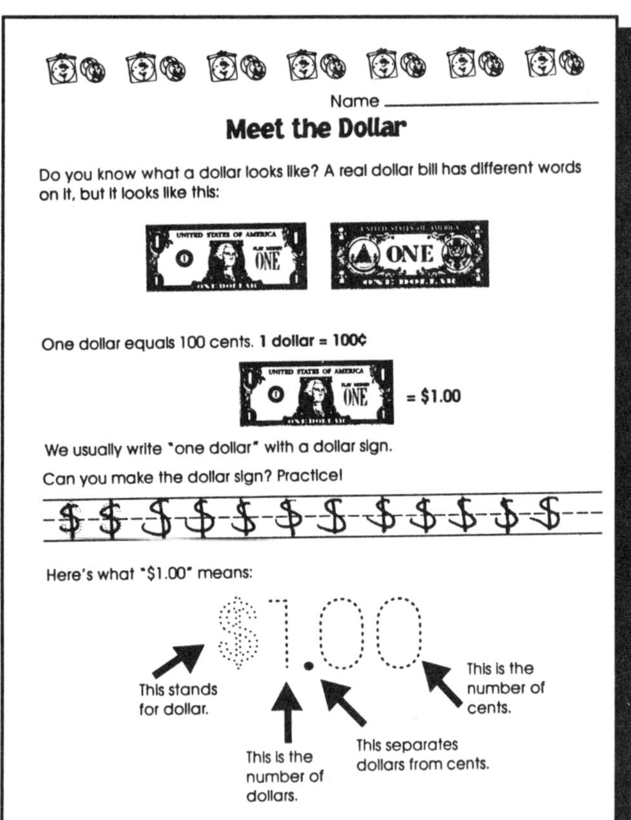

Name __________________

Meet the Dollar

Do you know what a dollar looks like? A real dollar bill has different words on it, but it looks like this:

One dollar equals 100 cents. **1 dollar = 100¢**

= $1.00

We usually write "one dollar" with a dollar sign.

Can you make the dollar sign? Practice!

$ $ $ $ $ $ $ $ $ $ $ $

Here's what "$1.00" means:

$1.00

This stands for dollar.

This is the number of dollars.

This separates dollars from cents.

This is the number of cents.

Page 60

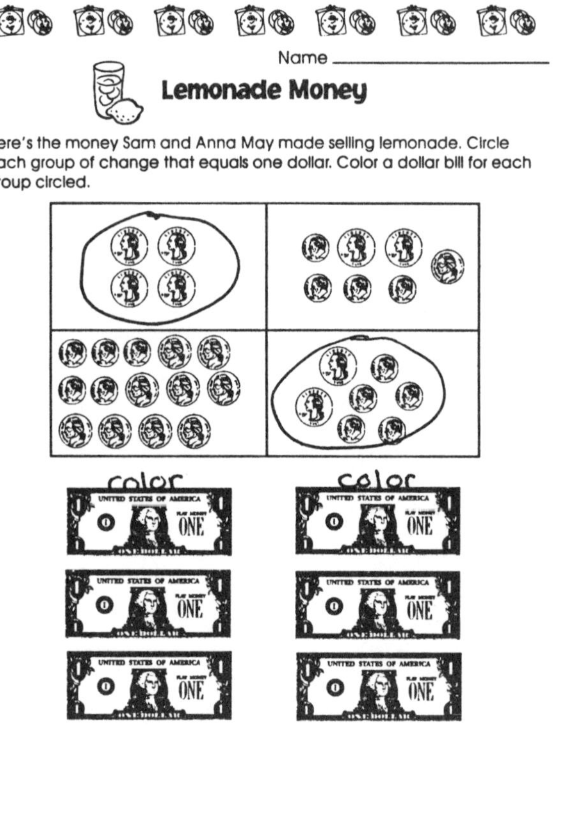

Name __________________

Lemonade Money

Here's the money Sam and Anna May made selling lemonade. Circle each group of change that equals one dollar. Color a dollar bill for each group circled.

color　　color

Page 61

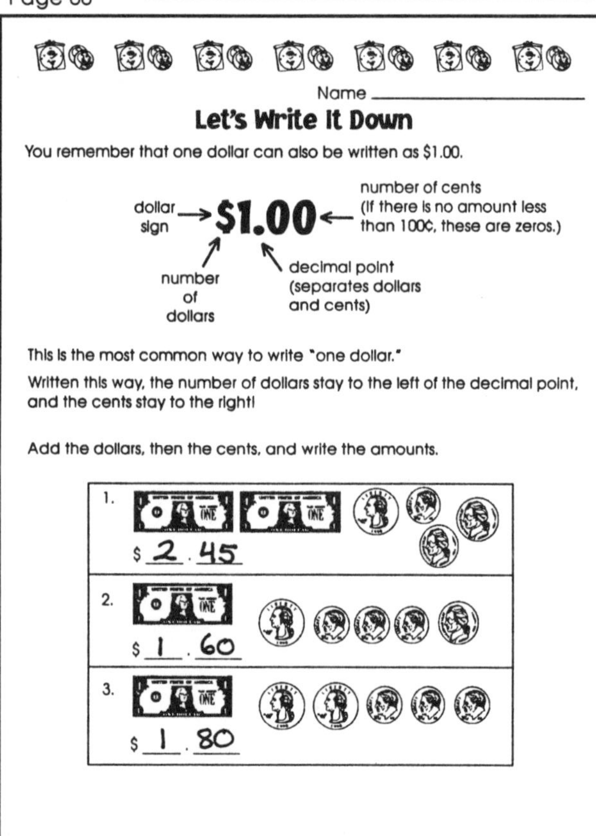

Name __________________

Let's Write It Down

You remember that one dollar can also be written as $1.00.

dollar sign → **$1.00** ← number of cents (If there is no amount less than 100¢, these are zeros.)

number of dollars

decimal point (separates dollars and cents)

This is the most common way to write "one dollar."

Written this way, the number of dollars stay to the left of the decimal point, and the cents stay to the right!

Add the dollars, then the cents, and write the amounts.

1. $ 2 . 45
2. $ 1 . 60
3. $ 1 . 80

Page 62

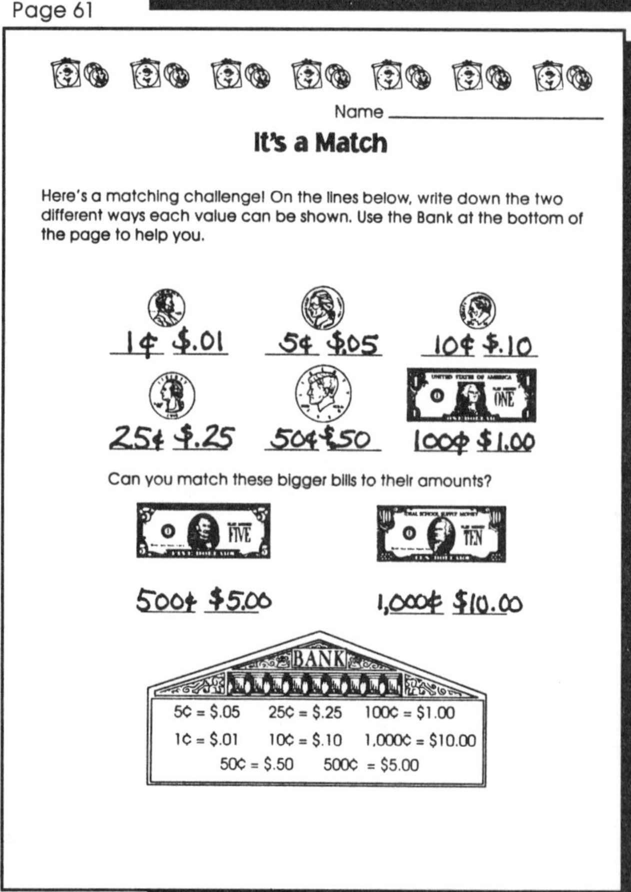

Name __________________

It's a Match

Here's a matching challenge! On the lines below, write down the two different ways each value can be shown. Use the Bank at the bottom of the page to help you.

1¢ $.01　　5¢ $.05　　10¢ $.10

25¢ $.25　　50¢ $.50　　100¢ $1.00

Can you match these bigger bills to their amounts?

500¢ $5.00　　1,000¢ $10.00

BANK

5¢ = $.05　　25¢ = $.25　　100¢ = $1.00

1¢ = $.01　　10¢ = $.10　　1,000¢ = $10.00

50¢ = $.50　　500¢ = $5.00

Page 63

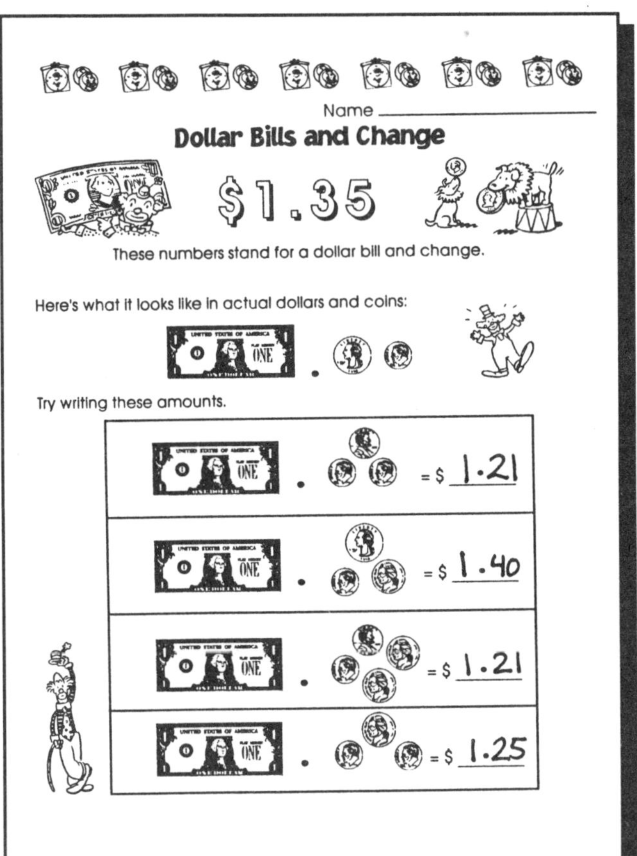

Name ______________

Dollar Bills and Change

$1.35

These numbers stand for a dollar bill and change.

Here's what it looks like in actual dollars and coins:

Try writing these amounts.

= $ 1.21

= $ 1.40

= $ 1.21

= $ 1.25

Page 64

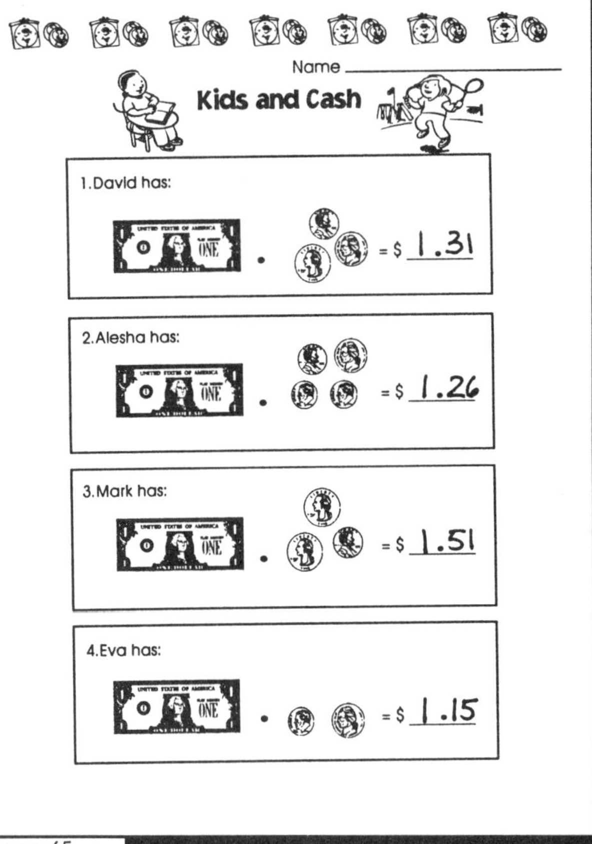

Name ______________

Kids and Cash

1. David has: = $ 1.31

2. Alesha has: = $ 1.26

3. Mark has: = $ 1.51

4. Eva has: = $ 1.15

Page 65

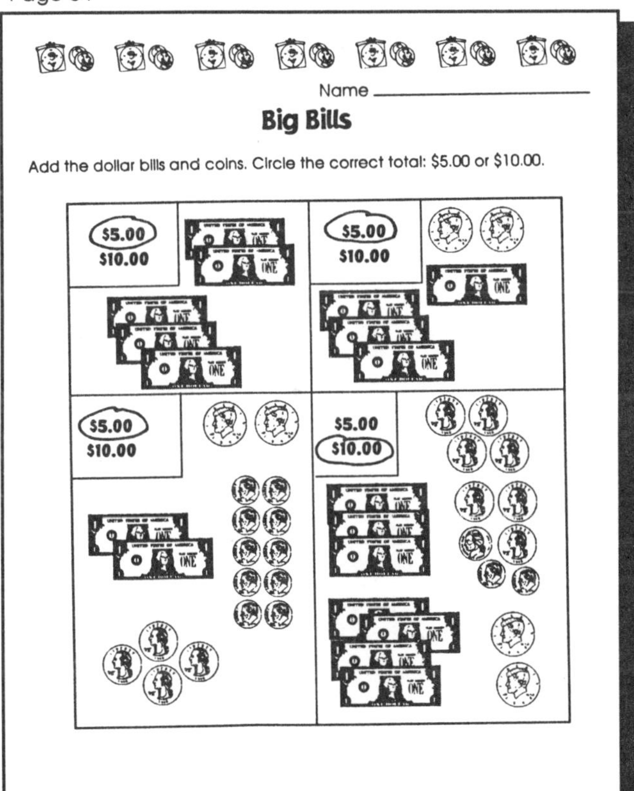

Name ______________

Big Bills

Add the dollar bills and coins. Circle the correct total: $5.00 or $10.00.

(**$5.00**) **$10.00**	**$5.00** (**$10.00**)...

(**$5.00**) **$10.00**

$10.00

(**$5.00**) **$10.00**

$5.00 (**$10.00**)

Page 66

Name ______________

Dollar Power

Adding dollars isn't any different than adding cents—but all the adding goes on in the dollar columns when there are no cents left over.

Here's an example.

$1.00
+ 5.00
$ 6.00

The total is in dollars only.

No cents means zeros in both cents columns.

Add these amounts. Regroup if you need to.

$10.00 + 1.00 = $11.00	$ 5.00 + 7.00 = $12.00	$ 3.00 + 9.00 = $12.00
$20.00 + 13.00 = $33.00	$ 9.00 + 11.00 = $20.00	$14.00 + 6.00 = $20.00
$ 7.00 + 6.00 = $13.00	$ 9.00 + 13.00 = $22.00	$16.00 + 8.00 = $24.00

Page 67

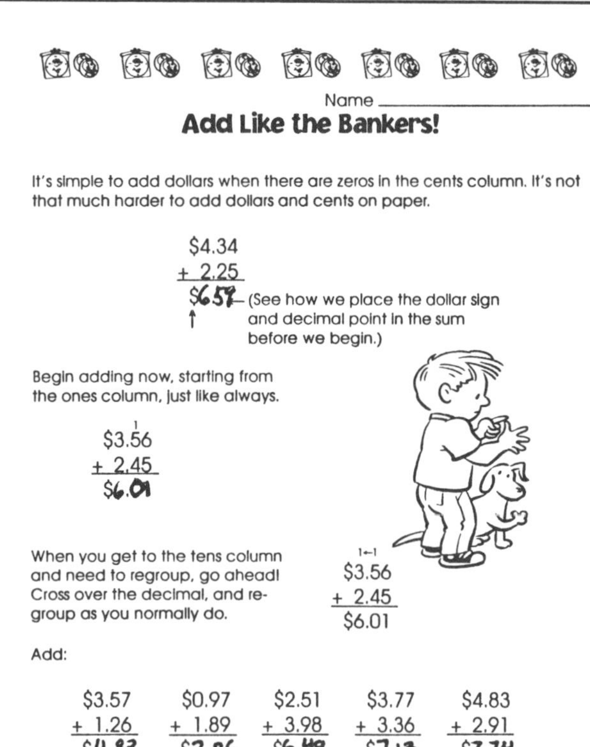

Name ______________

Add Like the Bankers!

It's simple to add dollars when there are zeros in the cents column. It's not that much harder to add dollars and cents on paper.

$4.34
+ 2.25
$6.59 ← (See how we place the dollar sign and decimal point in the sum before we begin.)

Begin adding now, starting from the ones column, just like always.

$3.56
+ 2.45
$6.01

When you get to the tens column and need to regroup, go ahead! Cross over the decimal, and regroup as you normally do.

$3.56
+ 2.45
$6.01

Add:

$3.57	$0.97	$2.51	$3.77	$4.83
+ 1.26	+ 1.89	+ 3.98	+ 3.36	+ 2.91
$4.83	$2.86	$6.49	$7.13	$7.74

Page 68

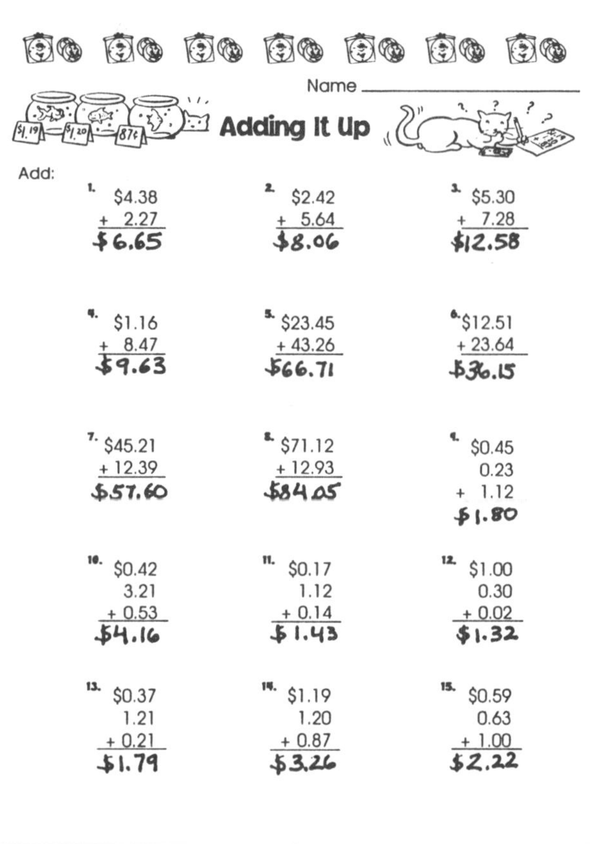

Name ______________

Adding It Up

Add:

1. $4.38 + 2.27 = $6.65	2. $2.42 + 5.64 = $8.06	3. $5.30 + 7.28 = $12.58
4. $1.16 + 8.47 = $9.63	5. $23.45 + 43.26 = $66.71	6. $12.51 + 23.64 = $36.15
7. $45.21 + 12.39 = $57.60	8. $71.12 + 12.93 = $84.05	9. $0.45 0.23 + 1.12 = $1.80
10. $0.42 3.21 + 0.53 = $4.16	11. $0.17 1.12 + 0.14 = $1.43	12. $1.00 0.30 + 0.02 = $1.32
13. $0.37 1.21 + 0.21 = $1.79	14. $1.19 1.20 + 0.87 = $3.26	15. $0.59 0.63 + 1.00 = $2.22

Page 69

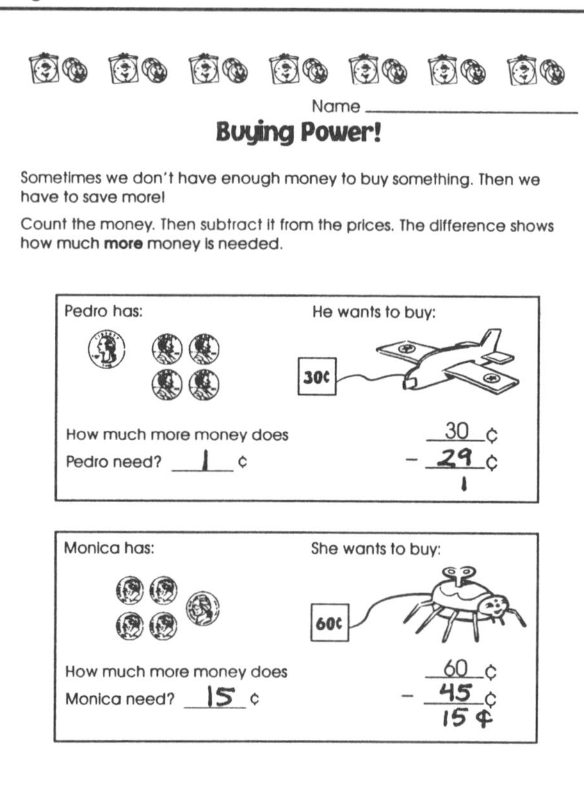

Name ______________

Buying Power!

Sometimes we don't have enough money to buy something. Then we have to save more!

Count the money. Then subtract it from the prices. The difference shows how much **more** money is needed.

Pedro has: He wants to buy: 30¢

How much more money does Pedro need? 1 ¢

30 ¢
− 29 ¢
1

Monica has: She wants to buy: 60¢

How much more money does Monica need? 15 ¢

60 ¢
− 45 ¢
15 ¢

Page 70

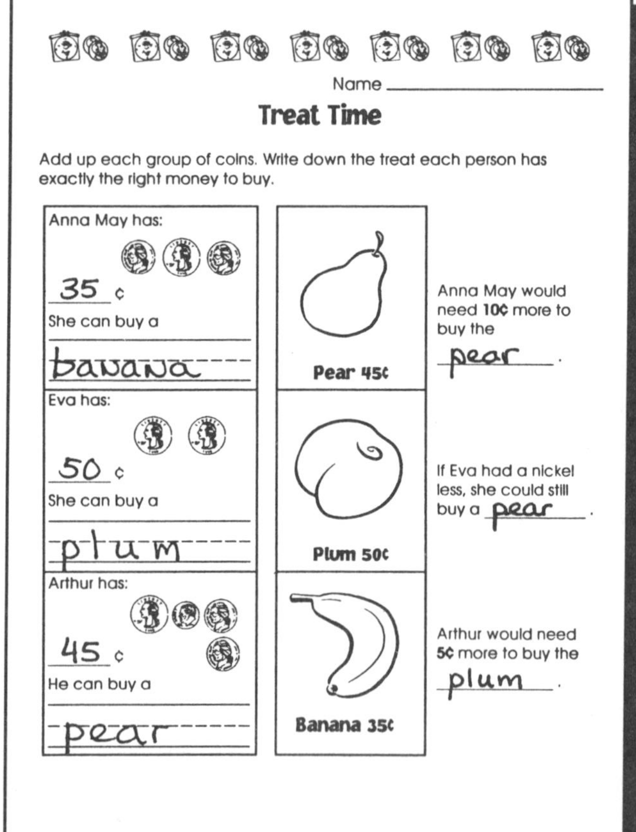

Name ______________

Treat Time

Add up each group of coins. Write down the treat each person has exactly the right money to buy.

Anna May has: 35 ¢ She can buy a banana	Pear 45¢	Anna May would need **10¢** more to buy the pear.
Eva has: 50 ¢ She can buy a plum	Plum 50¢	If Eva had a nickel less, she could still buy a pear.
Arthur has: 45 ¢ He can buy a pear	Banana 35¢	Arthur would need **5¢** more to buy the plum.

Page 71

Name ____________

Earning Money to Spend

Chung wants to buy her grandmother a special birthday present. She's been saving money for months! Help her add it up. **Hint:** You can carry over between dollars and cents, just like regular addition!

She started out with 3 quarters, or $0.75

She earned $1.00 raking leaves. $0.75 + $1.00 = $1.75

She traded in soda pop cans for 20¢. + $0.20 = $1.95

Chung walked Mrs. Ross's dog for 50¢. + $0.50 = $2.45

She made $2.00 selling lemondade. + $2.00 = $4.45

Chung found another quarter under her bed! + $0.25 = $4.70

Chung wants to buy a red, flowered scarf for $6.00.

Does she have enough money yet? Circle your answer.

Yes (No)

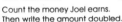

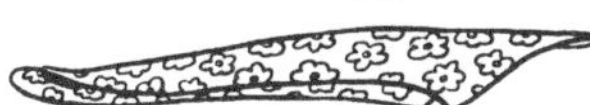

Page 72

Earning Money to Spend cont. Name ____________

David wants to buy a new leash for his dog Chiggles. The leash costs $5.00. Add David's money.

David had $2.15 in his bank. He was paid $1.00 for watering the garden. $2.15 + $1.00 = $3.15

David's father paid him $2.00 for weeding. + $2.00 = $5.15

He found a dime in the grass! + $0.10 = $5.25

Then David earned 50¢ for washing all the dishes. + $0.50 = $5.75

Can David buy the leash? (Yes) No

When David went to the pet store, he saw a nice rawide bone for 50¢. He would like to buy that and the leash.

David's money = $5.75
Leash = −$5.00
Money left over = $.75

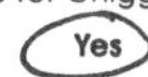

Can David buy the bone for Chiggles, too?

(Yes) No

Page 73

Name ____________

Double Your Money!

Joel wants to buy a new game for his computer. His grandmother says she will double any money that Joel earns.

Count the money Joel earns. Then write the amount doubled.

Joel's Jobs	Money Earned	Doubled
On Saturday, he cleaned the hall closet.	$ 0.30	$ 0.60
On Monday, he helped wash Mom's car.	$ 1.00	$ 2.00
On Tuesday, he couldn't find a job, but he found this on the sidewalk.	$ 0.25	$ 0.50
On Wednesday, Joel sold one of his baseball cards. 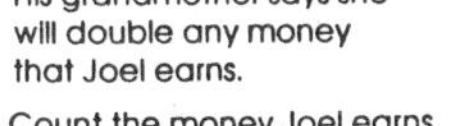	$ 0.75	$ 1.50

Page 74

Double Your Money! cont. Name ____________

Count the money Joel earns. Then write the amount doubled.

Joel's Jobs	Money Earned	Doubled
On Thursday, Joel took his aunt's dog for a walk.	$ 0.50	$ 1.00
On Friday, he helped Dad bake bread.	$ 0.60	$ 1.20
On Saturday, Joel cut the grass and watered the flowers.	$ 2.00	$ 4.00

Page 75

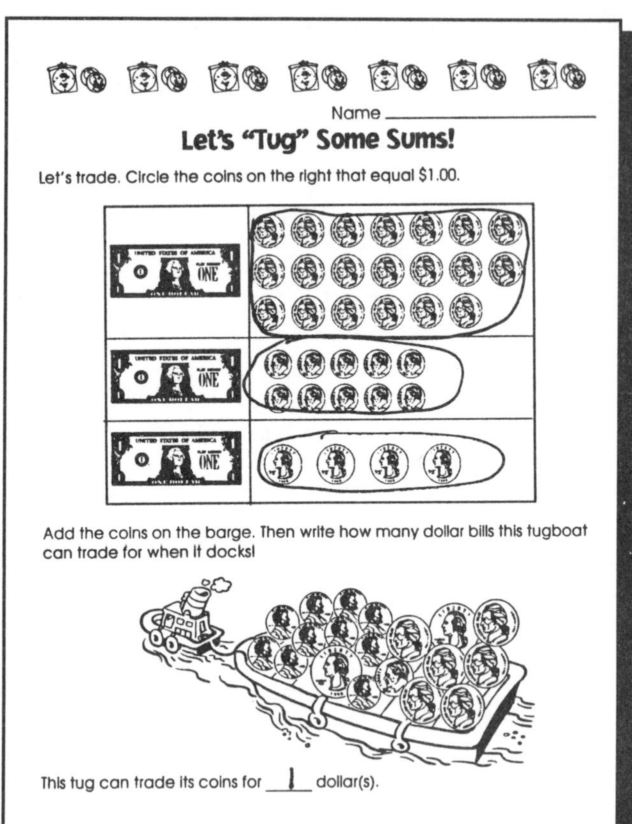

Name ____________

Let's "Tug" Some Sums!

Let's trade. Circle the coins on the right that equal $1.00.

Add the coins on the barge. Then write how many dollar bills this tugboat can trade for when it docks!

This tug can trade its coins for __1__ dollar(s).

Page 76

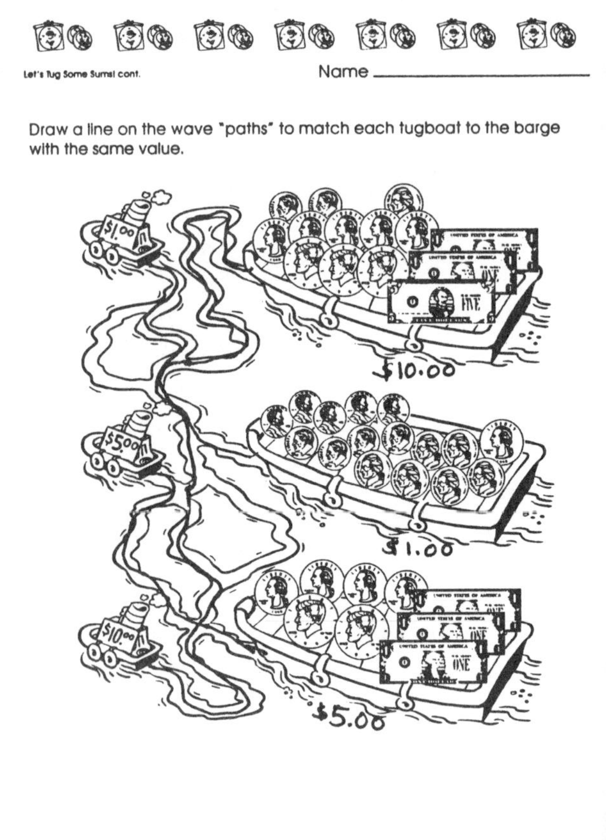

Let's Tug Some Sums! cont.

Name ____________

Draw a line on the wave "paths" to match each tugboat to the barge with the same value.

Page 77

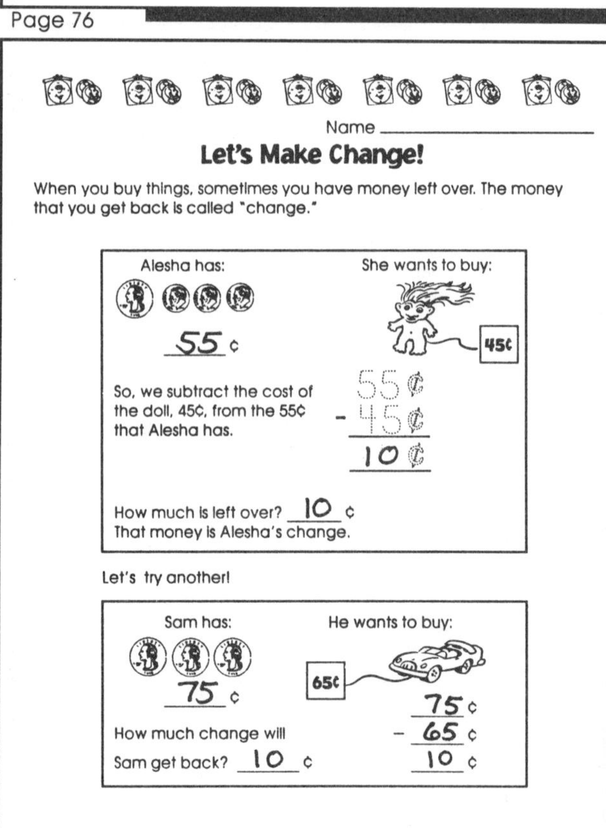

Name ____________

Let's Make Change!

When you buy things, sometimes you have money left over. The money that you get back is called "change."

Alesha has: __55__ ¢

She wants to buy: 45¢

So, we subtract the cost of the doll, 45¢, from the 55¢ that Alesha has.

55¢ − 45¢ = 10¢

How much is left over? __10__ ¢
That money is Alesha's change.

Let's try another!

Sam has: __75__ ¢

He wants to buy: 65¢

How much change will Sam get back? __10__ ¢

75¢ − 65¢ = 10¢

Page 78

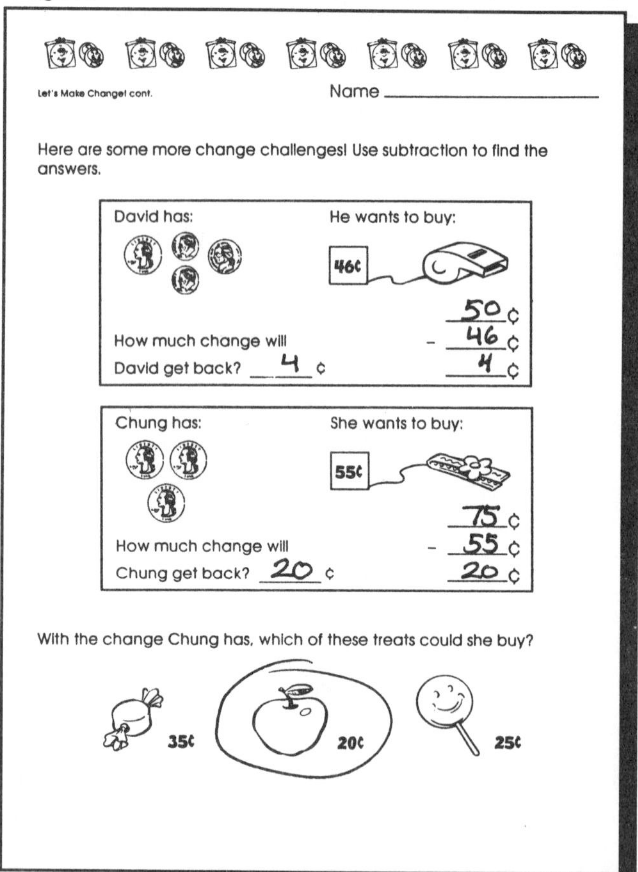

Let's Make Change! cont.

Name ____________

Here are some more change challenges! Use subtraction to find the answers.

David has:

He wants to buy: 46¢

How much change will David get back? __4__ ¢

50¢ − 46¢ = 4¢

Chung has:

She wants to buy: 55¢

How much change will Chung get back? __20__ ¢

75¢ − 55¢ = 20¢

With the change Chung has, which of these treats could she buy?

35¢ 20¢ 25¢

Page 79

Name ______________________

Changing Change

When we buy something, we are often given change back. To figure out change, we subtract.

Example:

Lindsey wants to buy a puzzle that costs $1.75.
She gives the cashier $2.00.
Should she get any money back?
Of course! It's her change.

Here's how it looks as a math problem.

$$\begin{array}{r} \$2.00 \\ -1.75 \\ \hline \$0.25 \end{array}$$

She gets back $0.25.

What will the cashier most likely give her in change?

one quarter 2 dimes 3 dimes

Martha went to the pet store to buy food for her hamster. It cost $4.25. Martha gave the cashier a five-dollar bill.

$$\begin{array}{r} \$5.00 \\ -4.25 \\ \hline \$0.75 \end{array}$$

Let's figure the change. What coins will she get back?
Circle any coin combinations she might be given. You will have more than one answer.

A. 2 quarters and 1dime
B. 7 dimes and 1 nickel
C. 2 quarters, 2 dimes, and 1 nickel
D. 1 half-dollar and 1 quarter
E. 3 quarters

Page 80

Name ______________________

Change Champs

Have each shopper choose the most expensive toy each one can buy. Then help them figure out their change. Write each shopper's name under the right toy.

Maria has $5.00.
Jonathan has $1.00.
David has $10.00.
Tony has $2.00.
Janesa has $9.00
Eva has $6.00.

$9.85 buyer: David	$0.78 buyer: Jonathon	$1.68 buyer: Tony
$4.98 buyer: Maria	$8.90 buyer: Janesa	$5.89 buyer: Eva

Maria: $5.00 − 4.98 = $ .02

Tony: $2.00 − 1.68 = $ .32

David: $10.00 − 9.85 = $ .15

Janesa: $9.00 − 8.90 = $ .10

Jonathan: $1.00 − .78 = $ .22

Eva: $6.00 − 5.89 = $ .11

Page 81

Name ______________________

Change Challenges

Time to go shopping. Help each student compute his or her change.

Let's figure the change for Martha's sunglasses.

1. Martha picks out some sunglasses.
The price is $9.40.
She hands the cashier a $10.00 bill.

$$\begin{array}{r} \$10.00 \\ -\ 9.40 \\ \hline \$\ .60 \end{array}$$

Now let's decide what the change should be!
Circle the correct coins:

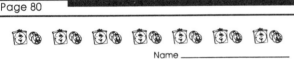

2. Maria picks out a stuffed tiger that costs $4.28.
She hands the cashier $4.50.

$$\begin{array}{r} \$\ 4.50 \\ -\ 4.28 \\ \hline \$\ .22 \end{array}$$

Circle the correct change.

Page 82

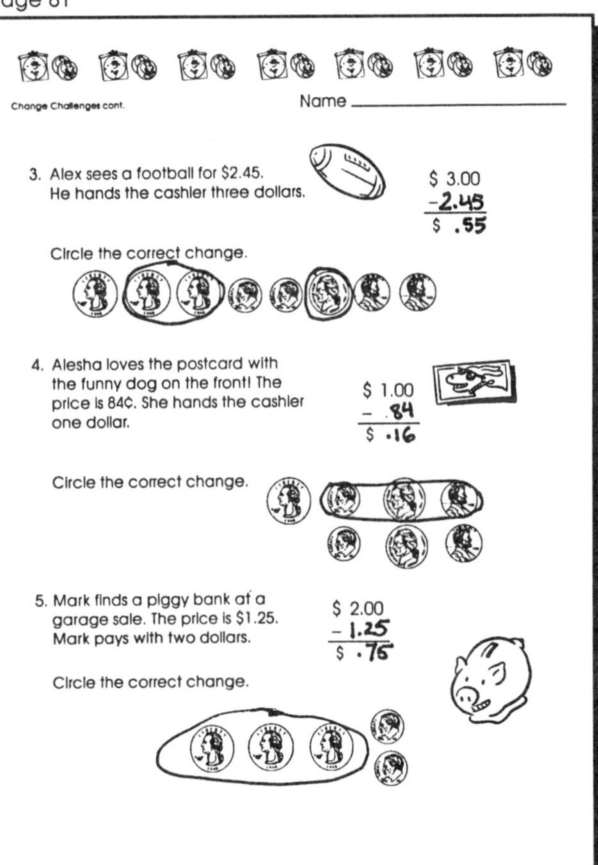

Change Challenges cont.

Name ______________________

3. Alex sees a football for $2.45.
He hands the cashier three dollars.

$$\begin{array}{r} \$\ 3.00 \\ -2.45 \\ \hline \$\ .55 \end{array}$$

Circle the correct change.

4. Alesha loves the postcard with the funny dog on the front! The price is 84¢. She hands the cashier one dollar.

$$\begin{array}{r} \$\ 1.00 \\ -\ .84 \\ \hline \$\ .16 \end{array}$$

Circle the correct change.

5. Mark finds a piggy bank at a garage sale. The price is $1.25. Mark pays with two dollars.

$$\begin{array}{r} \$\ 2.00 \\ -\ 1.25 \\ \hline \$\ .75 \end{array}$$

Circle the correct change.

Page 83

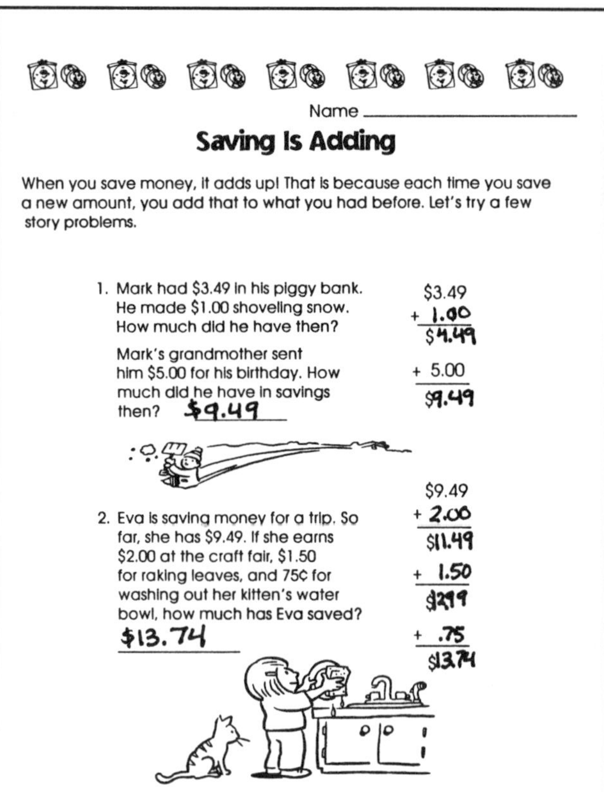

Name ____________

Saving Is Adding

When you save money, it adds up! That is because each time you save a new amount, you add that to what you had before. Let's try a few story problems.

1. Mark had $3.49 in his piggy bank. He made $1.00 shoveling snow. How much did he have then?

   $3.49 + 1.00 = $4.49

   Mark's grandmother sent him $5.00 for his birthday. How much did he have in savings then? **$9.49**

   + 5.00 = $9.49

2. Eva is saving money for a trip. So far, she has $9.49. If she earns $2.00 at the craft fair, $1.50 for raking leaves, and 75¢ for washing out her kitten's water bowl, how much has Eva saved? **$13.74**

   $9.49 + 2.00 = $11.49
   + 1.50 = $12.99
   + .75 = $13.74

Page 84

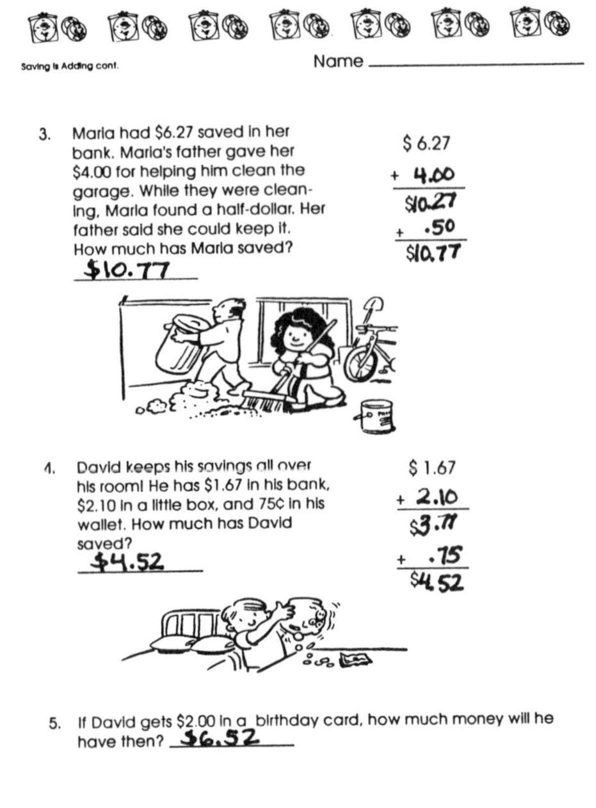

Saving Is Adding cont. Name ____________

3. Maria had $6.27 saved in her bank. Maria's father gave her $4.00 for helping him clean the garage. While they were cleaning, Maria found a half-dollar. Her father said she could keep it. How much has Maria saved? **$10.77**

   $6.27 + 4.00 = $10.27
   + .50 = $10.77

4. David keeps his savings all over his room! He has $1.67 in his bank, $2.10 in a little box, and 75¢ in his wallet. How much has David saved? **$4.52**

   $1.67 + 2.10 = $3.77
   + .75 = $4.52

5. If David gets $2.00 in a birthday card, how much money will he have then? **$6.52**

Page 85

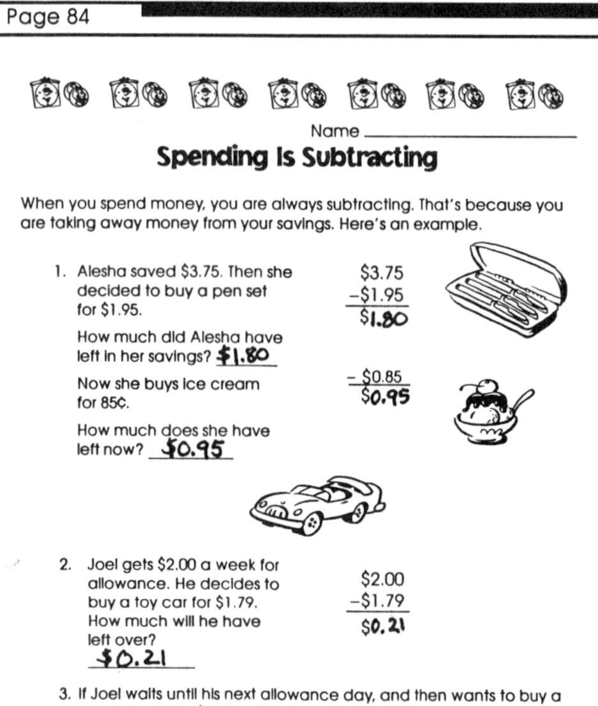

Name ____________

Spending Is Subtracting

When you spend money, you are always subtracting. That's because you are taking away money from your savings. Here's an example.

1. Alesha saved $3.75. Then she decided to buy a pen set for $1.95.

   $3.75 − $1.95 = $1.80

   How much did Alesha have left in her savings? **$1.80**

   Now she buys ice cream for 85¢.

   − $0.85 = $0.95

   How much does she have left now? **$0.95**

2. Joel gets $2.00 a week for allowance. He decides to buy a toy car for $1.79. How much will he have left over? **$0.21**

   $2.00 − $1.79 = $0.21

3. If Joel waits until his next allowance day, and then wants to buy a comic book for $2.25, will he be able to do it?

   Yes **(no)**

Page 86

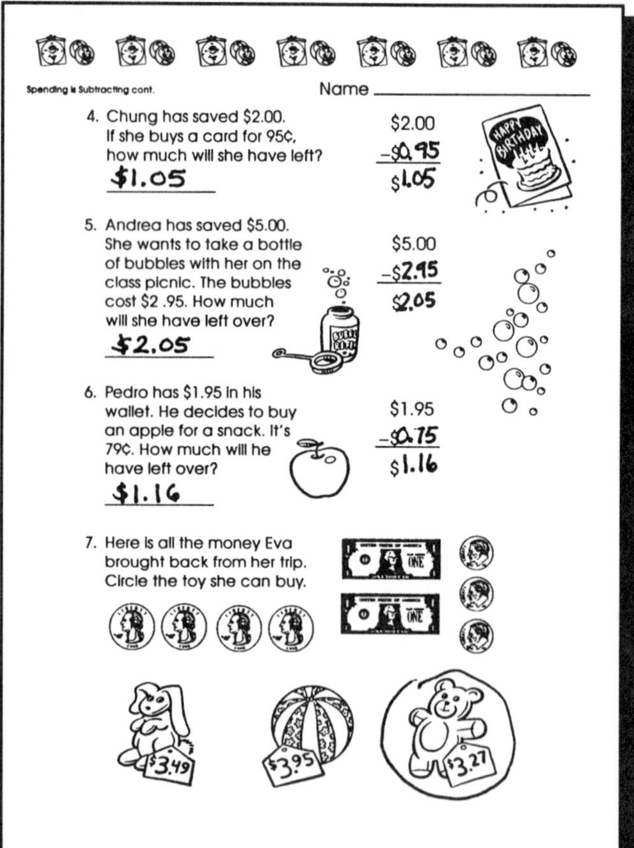

Spending Is Subtracting cont. Name ____________

4. Chung has saved $2.00. If she buys a card for 95¢, how much will she have left? **$1.05**

   $2.00 − $0.95 = $1.05

5. Andrea has saved $5.00. She wants to take a bottle of bubbles with her on the class picnic. The bubbles cost $2 .95. How much will she have left over? **$2.05**

   $5.00 − $2.95 = $2.05

6. Pedro has $1.95 in his wallet. He decides to buy an apple for a snack. It's 79¢. How much will he have left over? **$1.16**

   $1.95 − $0.75 = $1.16

7. Here is all the money Eva brought back from her trip. Circle the toy she can buy.

   $3.49 $3.95 **($3.27)**

Page 87

Name

Subtraction Detectives

Here's a fun challenge! Let's find out what each third-grader bought. The table shows how much money each student had to spend.

David	$20.00
Samantha	$20.00
Steven	$20.00
Christina	$10.00
Mark	$10.00
Andrea	$10.00

Your only clue is how much change each student had after his or her purchase!

Here are the items that David, Samantha, and Steven bought. When you figure out who bought what, write each name in the box underneath the correct item.

$15.50	$19.75	$8.75
Samantha	Steven	David

David	Samantha	Steven
$20.00 - 8.75 $11.25	$ 20.00 - 15.50 $ 4.50	$ 20.00 - 19.75 $ 0.25

Page 88

Subtraction Detectives cont.

Name

Here are the items that Christina, Mark, and Andrea bought. When you figure out who bought what, write each name in the box underneath the correct item.

$9.90	$7.50	$5.00
Andrea	Christina	Mark

Christina	Mark	Andrea
$ 10.00 - 7.50 $2.50	$ 10.00 - 5.00 $ 5.00	$ 10.00 - 9.90 $ 0.10

Of the six students:

1. Who spent the least money? Mark
2. Who spent the most money? Steven
3. Who got back the smallest amount of change? Andrea
4. Who got back the largest amount of change? David
5. What would you have bought from the items shown? Answers will vary.
6. Who bought your favorite item? ________

Page 89

Name

Spending and Saving

As we save and spend money, we have to add and subtract all the time. This is so we can keep track of how much money we have.

Add and subtract to find the answers.

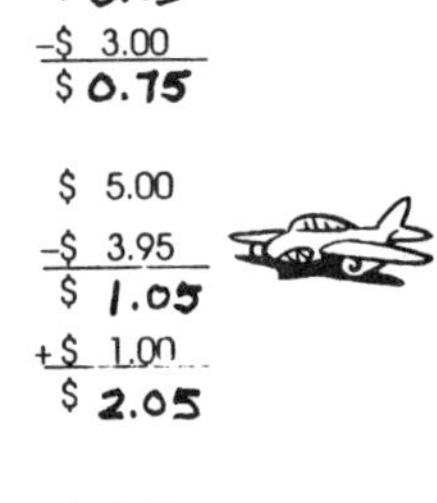

1. Monica saved $2.50. Then she earned another $1.25. Monica was invited to Maria's birthday party. She spent $3.00 on Maria's gift. What does she have left over? $0.75

   $ 2.50 + $ 1.25 = $ 3.75; − $ 3.00 = $ 0.75

2. David got $5.00 for his birthday. On a field trip, he spent $3.95 for a model of a plane. Then he earned $1.00 by helping his aunt in her yard. How much money does David have now? $2.05

   $ 5.00 − $ 3.95 = $ 1.05; + $ 1.00 = $ 2.05

3. Jason's uncle gave him $3.00 as a gift. Jason had saved $10.00. He decided to buy a paint set for $12.95. How much does Jason have left? $0.05

   $ 3.00 + $ 10.00 = $ 13.00; − $ 12.95 = $ 0.05

Page 90

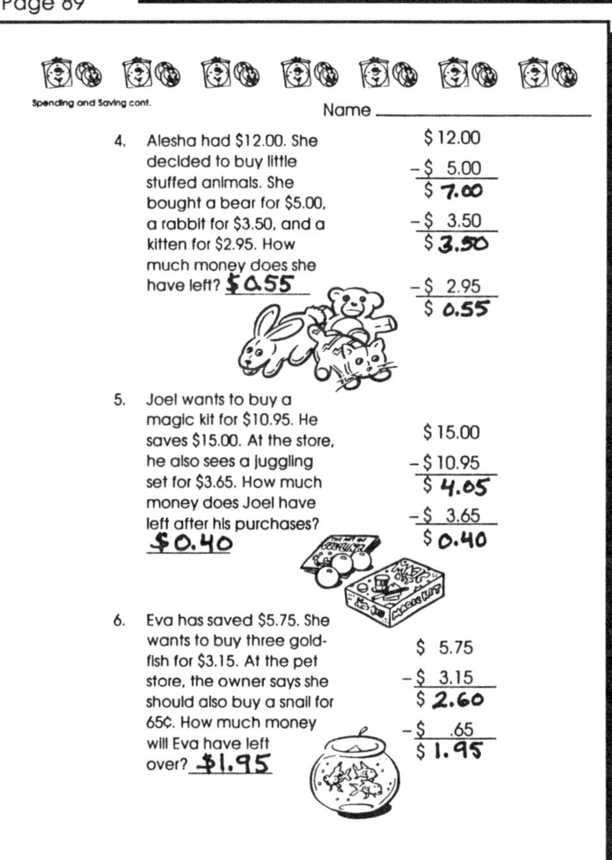

Spending and Saving cont.

Name

4. Alesha had $12.00. She decided to buy little stuffed animals. She bought a bear for $5.00, a rabbit for $3.50, and a kitten for $2.95. How much money does she have left? $0.55

   $ 12.00 − $ 5.00 = $ 7.00; − $ 3.50 = $ 3.50; − $ 2.95 = $ 0.55

5. Joel wants to buy a magic kit for $10.95. He saves $15.00. At the store, he also sees a juggling set for $3.65. How much money does Joel have left after his purchases? $0.40

   $ 15.00 − $ 10.95 = $ 4.05; − $ 3.65 = $ 0.40

6. Eva has saved $5.75. She wants to buy three goldfish for $3.15. At the pet store, the owner says she should also buy a snail for 65¢. How much money will Eva have left over? $1.95

   $ 5.75 − $ 3.15 = $ 2.60; − $ .65 = $ 1.95

Page 91

Name ____________

Up and Down

Larger amounts of money are made of paper.

Smaller amounts of money are made as coins.

Both can be used to trade for things of value. Find each sum. Circle the side of the teeter-totter that will fall. The side with the greater amount will go down.

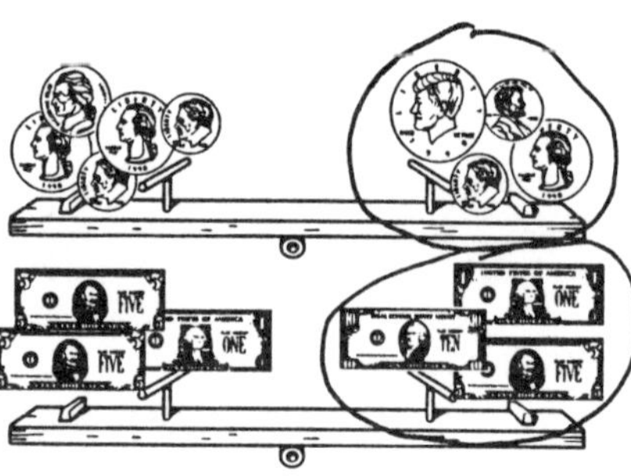

Page 92

Name ____________

Let's Compare!

Add each pair of sums. Circle the side with the greater amount.

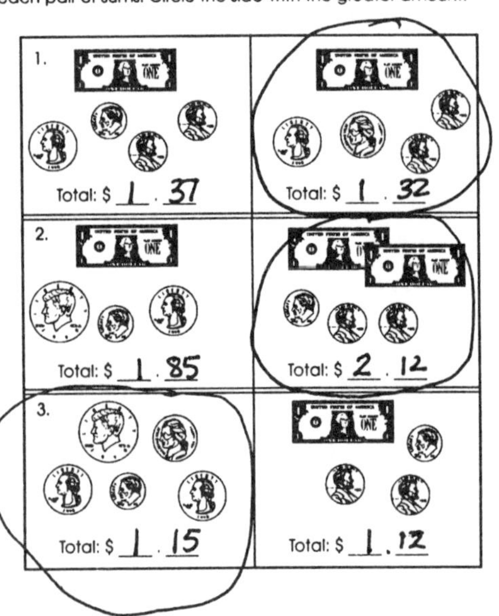

Page 93

Name ____________

The Art of Estimation

Estimation makes it much easier to add or subtract in your head. You can estimate by rounding numbers out to the nearest tens place. Numbers below 5 should be rounded down, and numbers of 5 and above should be rounded up. Example: Round 26¢ to 30¢.

These are on sale today in the lunchroom.

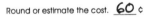

You have this money: 

You want the pizza.

Round or estimate the cost. 60 ¢

Do you have enough money? Yes (No)

The banana and the cookie look good!

Add the estimated prices. 20 + 10 = 30

Do you have enough money?

(Yes) No

Page 94

Name ____________

Line Up for Lunch

David has this money:

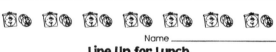

He has 60 cents.

He wants to buy milk and a banana to go with his sandwich from home.

If he buys milk , will he have enough left to buy the banana ?

(Yes) No

David's money = 60 ¢

Estimate the milk price − 40 ¢

He has about this much left over. 20 ¢

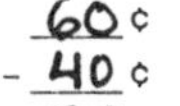

Eva has this money: 

She wants to buy the milk and something else to eat. Estimate to see if she has enough for milk and pizza.

Estimate the milk price 40¢

Estimate the pizza price 60¢

Does she have enough for both?

Yes (No)

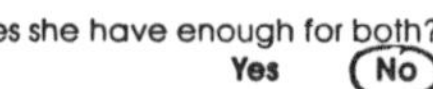

The cafeteria also has hot dogs on sale for 29¢ each. Estimate the hot dog price 30¢

Can Eva buy milk and a hot dog? (Yes) No

Page 95

Name ______________

Let's Estimate!

Sometimes we need to make a quick guess about money. So, we estimate!

> **Example:**
> Anthony sees a little car for 88¢.
> He thinks: "That's about 90¢!
> I have 90¢. Good, I can buy it!"

Circle the correct answers.

1. Mark sees a pinwheel for sale.
   It costs 79¢. That's about:

   60¢ 70¢ (80¢)

   He has 91¢.
   Does he have enough?

   (Yes) No

2. Lee wants to buy a bracelet.
   It costs 68¢. That's about:

   60¢ (70¢) 80¢

   She has 50¢.
   About how much more does Lee need?

   10¢ (20¢) 30¢ 40¢

   If Lee's mother gave her another 50¢ and Lee bought the bracelet, would she have enough money to buy a pinwheel, too?

   Yes (No)

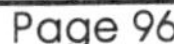

Page 96

Let's Estimate cont.

Name ______________

3. Earl wants to buy a toy car.
   It costs $1.39. That's about

   $1.30 ($1.40) $1.50

   He has $1.75.
   Does he have enough?

   (Yes) No

4. Chung would like to buy a hot dog. It costs 57¢.
   That's about:

   (60¢) 50¢ 70¢

   She has 65¢.
   Does she have enough?

   (Yes) No

5. Eva sees a ball that she really likes. It costs $2.49.
   That's about:

   $2.00 ($2.50) $3.00

   She has $3.00.
   Does she have enough?

   (Yes) No

6. David wants to buy a new pen.
   It costs $2.89. That's about

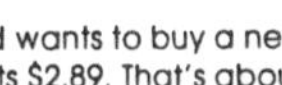

   $2.00 $2.50 ($3.00)

   He has $2.75.
   Does he have enough?

   Yes (No)

Page 97

Name ______________

Estimate Away!

When we want to know if our addition is close, we simply estimate.

If the real amounts are:	We round to the nearest ten cents:	
$0.84	$0.80	(4 or less, round down.)
−$0.25	−$0.30	(5 or more, round up.)
$1.09	$1.10	

Does our estimate look close? Yes! Then, it's probably right!

Let's try another problem!

If the real amounts are:	We round to the nearest ten cents:
$0.34	$0.30
+$0.21	+$0.20
$0.55	$0.50

Are we close? Yes! Good! Then it's probably right!

Make a quick estimate on these problems:

1.		2.	
$0.67	$0.70	$0.52	$0.50
+$0.32	+$0.30	+$0.86	+$0.90
$0.99	$1.00	$1.38	$1.40

Were you close? yes

Page 98

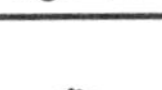       

Estimate Away cont.

Name ______________

Estimate each sum. If your sum is close, star your answer. If it is not close, add the original equation again to get the correct answer.

	Real amounts	Estimate	Try again:
3.	$0.38	$0.40	_____
	+$0.24	+$0.20	+ _____
	$0.62	$0.60	
4.	$0.84	$0.80	_____
	+$0.36	+$0.40	+ _____
	$1.20	$1.20	
5.	$0.21	$0.20	_____
	$0.53	$0.50	_____
	+$0.36	+$0.40	+ _____
	$1.10	$1.10	
6.	$0.37	$0.40	_____
	$0.52	$0.50	_____
	+$0.22	+0.20	+ _____
	$1.11	$1.10	

Page 99

Name ______________________

Shopping in the Next Galaxy

Mrs. Bleepz goes to the Zotz Market for her groceries. Her children—Blurp, Zeezo, and Bleeza—go with her.

1. Mrs. Bleepz asks Bleeza to pick out the galactic juice. She says, "Find a brand that costs less than $1.00 a gallon."

   Circle the galactic juice Bleeza picks.

   Starshine Berry
   3 gallons/$3.00

   Galaxy Grape
   2 gallons/$1.95

   Transport Treat
   2 gallons/$2.00

2. Mrs. Bleepz sends Blurp to buy sand-snake stew, but she wants a brand that costs $1.00 a can.

   Circle Blurp's choice of stew.

   Snazzy Snake
   2 cans for
   $3.50

   Slinky Stew
   2 cans for
   $2.00

   Can-O-Viper
   2 cans for
   $2.25

3. Zeezo has to find mudwort muffins that are 25¢ each.

   Circle the brand he chooses.

   Wort Wonders
   4 for $4.00

   Mud Muffins
   4 for $1.00

   Best Mud
   4 for $2.00

Page 100

Shopping in the Next Galaxy cont.

Name ______________________

4. Mrs. Bleepz tells each of her children they can each have a treat, and gives them $3.00 to divide.

   Circle a choice for each kid. The treats must add up to exactly $3.00.

Bleeza:	Grummi Snakes $0.75	Caramel Sand Beetle $1.05	Galactic Gum $0.90
Blurp:	Snake-sicle $0.90	Grape Goo $1.25	Desert Toad Treat $1.15
Zeezo:	Wortberry Tarts $0.85	ZapDrops $1.00	Plutonic Bar $1.35

5. At the checkout lane, all of Mrs. Bleepz's groceries add up to $22.85.

   She hands the cashier:   

   Calculate her change: $ 25.00
   \- 22.85
   $ 2.15

   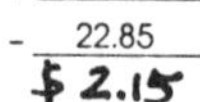

6. Blurp sees a Desert Dragon comic book he wants. Can Mrs. Bleepz buy it with her change?

   Yes No

Page 101

Name ______________________

The Money Challenge!

Work your way down this challenging path! Earn your way to the finish line!

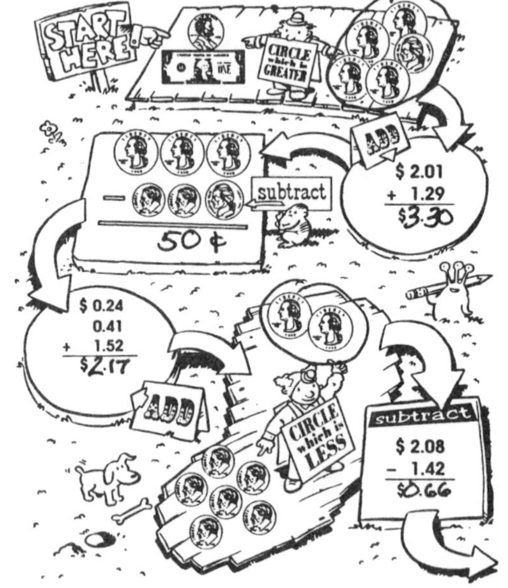

Page 102

The Money Challenge! cont.

Name ______________________

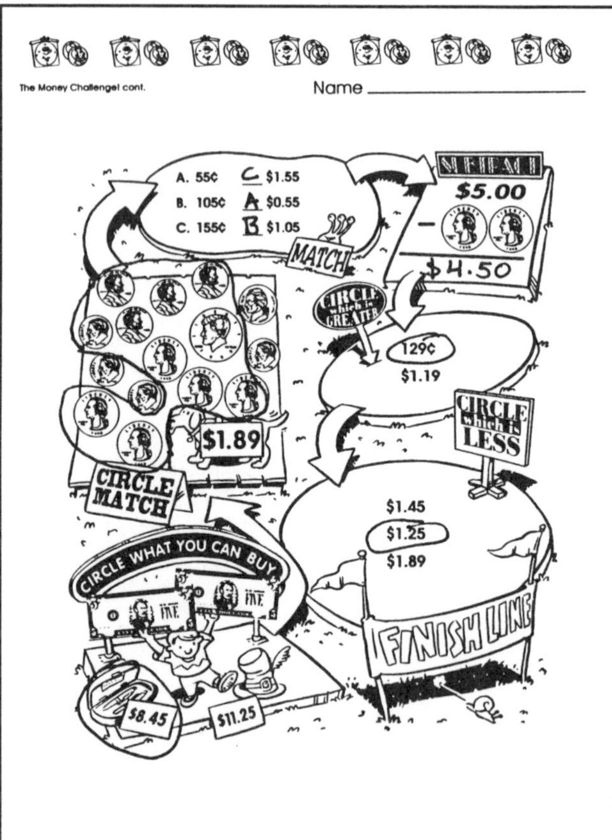

Page 103